CLASSIC
ROCK

CLASSIC
ROCK

GARY CEE

MetroBooks

MetroBooks

AN IMPRINT OF FRIEDMAN/FAIRFAX PUBLISHERS

Library of Congress Cataloging-in-Publication Data
Cee, Gary
    Classic rock / Gary Cee.
        p. cm.
    Includes bibligraphical references
    ISBN 1-56799-168-8
    1. Rock Music--1961-1970-- History and criticism. 2 Rock
music--1971-1980-- History and criticism. I. Title.
ML3534.C43 1995
781.66'09--dc20

                                                                95-1496
                                                                  CIP
                                                                  MN

Editor: Susan Lauzau
Art Director: Jeff Batzli
Designer: Andrea Karman
Photography Editor: Emilya Naymark

Pre – press by Ocean Graphic International Company Ltd.
Printed in China by Leefung-Asco Printers Ltd.

For bulk purchases and special sales, please contact:
Friedman/Fairfax Publishers
Attention: Sales Department
15 West 26th Street
New York, NY 10010
212/685-6610 FAX 212/685-1307

ACKNOWLEDGMENTS

The author expresses sincere gratitude to:

Mordechai Kleidermacher, for taking countless phone calls

and knowing more about classic rock than a human should.

Gary Schulman, for knowing where to draw the line.

Lou O'Neill, Jr., for loving rock and roll more than anyone I know.

Sharyn Rosart, for giving me the opportunity to write this book.

And many thanks to: Susan Lauzau, Nathaniel Marunas, Frank Garritano, Traie Owens,

Eric and Seija Flaum, Kathy Kleidermacher, Alan Cohn, Tom Cording, Chris King,

Tom Calderone, John Loscalzo, Donna Donna, Malibu Sue, Jodi Vale, Maria Marchetti, Chris Cassidy,

Evan Davies,Russ Mottla, Linda Pitt, Dennis Daniel, Brian Cosgrove, Hillary Blazer, Debe Black, Dah Zako,

Ron Morey, Gary Victor, Lani Zarief, Michael Renchiwich, Gerald Rothberg, Lydia Sherwood,

Paul Jacobs, Ida Langsam, Katherine Turman, Jeff Kitts, David Fricke, Jesse Dylan,

Joey Ramone, Gene Simmons, the late Frank Zappa, the Melzers,

and especially, the Sweda family—Jeanne, Chip, Raegen, and JT.

The biggest thanks of all to Marjorie and John, Mom and Pop, for letting me blast the stereo.

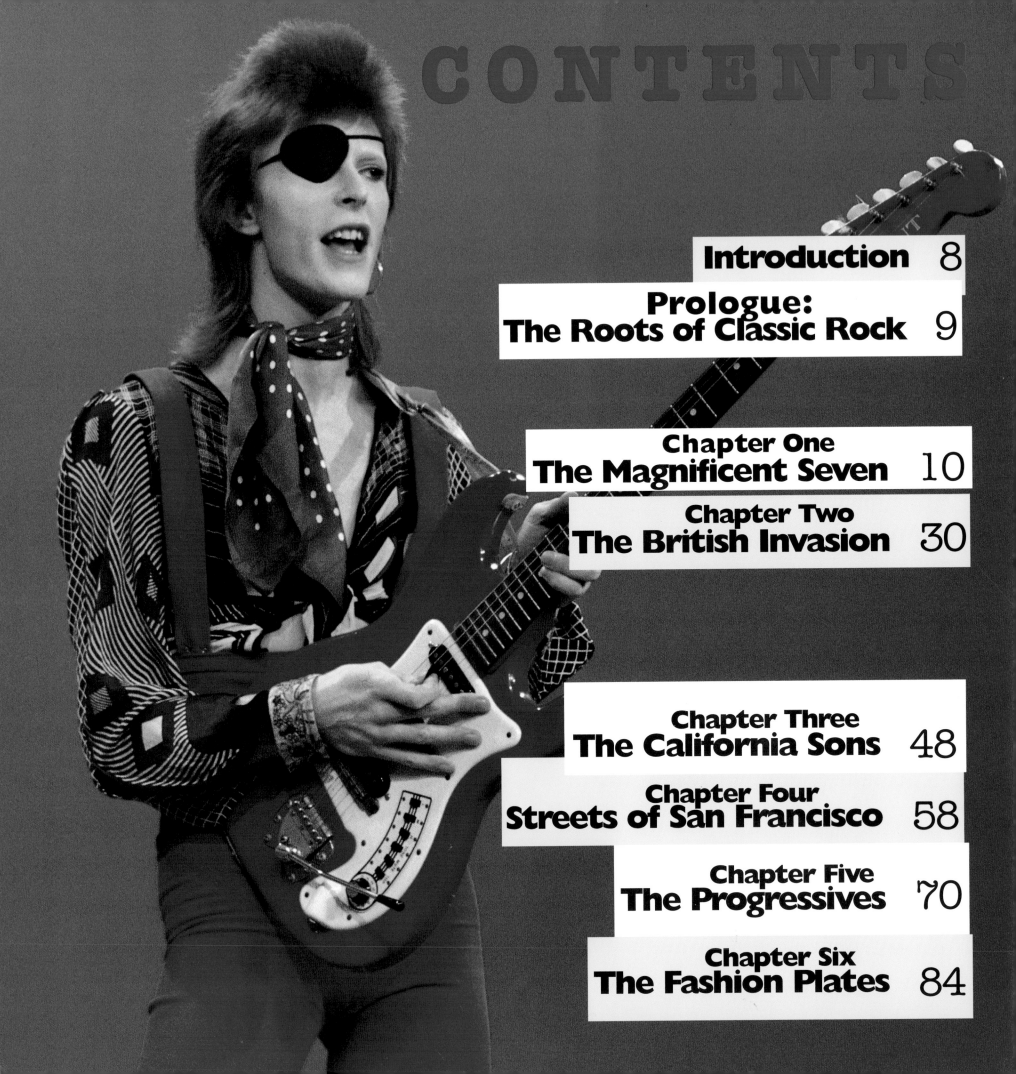

CONTENTS

Introduction

By Pete Fornatale

The sounds are unforgettable.

The images are indestructible.

The impact is inescapable.

Classic rock has accompanied us on the journey from innocence to experience; the revolutionary political and social movements of the sixties and seventies are now part of history. And the music that played behind it all is chiseled into our collective consciousness.

But rock 'n' roll actually has its origins in other eras, other countries, other cultures. It stole with discretion, taking only from the very best the world of music had to offer—bits of the blues, folk, country, jazz, pop, and even gospel and classical. The rock 'n' roll revolution started out like distant thunder, a blip on the radar screen that was surely no threat to the established order. But then the drums grew louder and the beat got stronger and the raw, seductive power of the music could not be denied. Like a blade of grass that somehow manages to penetrate concrete, early rock grew fast and wild, quickly smothering more staid forms of entertainment.

Then a funny thing happened. As the kids who loved rock 'n'roll grew up, so did the music. It expanded. It evolved. It embraced weighty issues and worldly themes. Rock 'n' roll collided with the sixties. A special brand of music—what we know as classic rock— was born in the fire of that tumultuous decade. If ever the medium *was* the message, this was it. No matter what the titles of the songs or content of the lyrics, the essential meaning of rock came through: freedom, ecstasy, peace, and even, for some, God. In the words of those who lived it—and recorded it—take it as it comes, we can work it out, we want the world and we want it now, let it bleed, let it be....

In its best moments classic rock is sex, love, politics, and religion all rock 'n' rolled into one. All aspects of life in the latter half of the twentieth century have been touched by its power and marked by its fury. And classic rock remains challenging, life affirming, and downright fun.

Admittedly, though, some things have changed along the way. In the beginning, rock benefitted greatly from the element of surprise; the fact that so much new and exciting music was pouring out of our stereos at such a breakneck pace was exhilarating. It seemed as if every day some new song or group was unlocking another key piece that we could use to figure out the puzzles of our lives.

But then another astonishing thing happened. Thirty years passed in the blink of an eye. There are no surprises in classic rock; instead there is familiarity and consistency. Classic rock offers us a comforting touchstone in an ever-changing world. Not a bad tradeoff, if you ask me. The emotional connection with the music is unbreakable. It's the difference between mere infatuation and long-lasting love.

I'd like to address one final point. There is a tendency in some quarters to denigrate classic rock, to deny its importance and minimize its overall relevance. After all, the argument goes, it's old hat. It's for dinosaurs. Youth must be served. Rock must remain rebellious and anti-establishment, and so on. Don't believe it for a second.

For one thing, most young people love classic rock. It was, and is, great music that they missed by a mere accident of birth. But even viewed as the eternal conflict between younger and older generations, listen to the wisdom of renowned author and psychiatrist Viktor E. Frankel. In a passage describing why young people should envy older people, he wrote, "Instead of possibilities in the future, they have realities in the past—the potentialities they have actualized, the meanings they have fulfilled, the value they have realized—and nothing and nobody can ever remove these assets from the past."

The same is true of classic rock. It reminds us of who we are and where we came from. It tells us we have survived and triumphed. Pop culture by its very nature is ephemeral. But some of it clings to the mind and sticks in the heart. If you still don't believe me, read the rest of this book. And while you're at it, turn on the nearest classic rock radio station and crank up the volume. The conclusions are obvious:

The sounds are unforgettable.

The images are indestructible.

The impact is inescapable.

PROLOGUE: THE ROOTS OF CLASSIC ROCK

When was rock and roll born? Good luck answering that question.

Rock and roll wasn't born as much as it evolved. Most agree that it began when Bill Haley & His Comets recorded "(We're Gonna) Rock Around the Clock" on April 12, 1954. The song was released a month later on the Decca label as the B side to Haley's "Thirteen Women," but to initial meager acceptance. A year later it opened *The Blackboard Jungle,* a Glenn Ford film about juvenile delinquents that was a big box-office hit with the teen set. So the single was rereleased, this time as an A side, and it climbed all the way to number one in July 1955, where it presided until September—quite a run. The floodgates of rock were opened.

Others insist that rock began further back than Haley's single. Jim Dawson and Steve Propes—authors of a book called *What Was the First Rock 'n' Roll Record?*—offer fifty candidates, the earliest being "Blues, Part 2," a 1944 recording by Jazz at the Philharmonic. But if you're going back that far, why stop there?

This much is more or less agreed on: rock and roll was spawned by rhythm and blues, which is rooted in jazz and country boogie, which was born from western swing, ragtime, and delta blues, which came from minstrel songs and church music from the turn of the twentieth century.

Parents prayed rock and roll would be only a passing fancy, but unless it's a forty-year fad, this music is not going away anytime soon. Four decades after Haley hit number one, rock and roll continues to diverge down a countless number of paths into one subgenre after another.

This book is about classic rock, a term dreamed up, for the most part, by radio station programmers to classify the body of electric guitar–driven popular music that began to flourish in the early sixties. Classic rock radio asserts, "It doesn't have to be old to be a classic," but most of its playlists rely on the heavyweights from the British invasion, the California sons, the psychedelics and progressives, the fashion plates, the folkies, the barroom and southern swingers, and the hard rockers of the mid- to late seventies.

Music is evocative of other times and places. Turn on the radio, hear a certain song, and soon you'll be carried back to your first kiss, or the summer you got your driver's license, or that blowout party you threw in college. The words and pictures in this book are meant to do the same, so sit back and let yourself be transported.

CHAPTER ONE

THE MAGNIFICENT SEVEN

Classic rock is loaded with pioneers, hangers-on, and copycats. Then there's another breed: the visionaries— an esteemed, courageous crew who stuck to their guns and never took no for an answer while building their empire.

Whatever their other similarities or differences, the musicians featured in this chapter shared a profound commitment to their vision and an unshakable belief in the character and integrity of their music. Their deeply personal statements broke from a caged existence as minority culture and crossed the boundaries into the popular consciousness. Eventually their mutations of the genre became standard, leaving indelible imprints on those who followed.

Decades later, their records spin in eternal rotation on classic rock radio stations. These few stand head and shoulders above the pack. Without them, all the other acts would have had a tougher go.

Let's call them the Magnificent Seven: the Beatles, the Rolling Stones, the Who, the Doors, Jimi Hendrix, Pink Floyd, and Led Zeppelin. Let the arguments begin! What about so-and-so? Possibly, the next best thing to enjoying music is quarreling over it.

The Who's Roger Daltrey; Mick Jagger of the Rolling Stones; Jimi Hendrix.

THE BEATLES

They were at the right place at the right time and were the perfect men for the job. The arrival of the Beatles from London at New York's Kennedy Airport at 1:35 on the afternoon of Friday, February 7, 1964, not only kicked off their first tour of America, it marked the starting point of the classic rock years.

The Beatles were simply the greatest and most famous rock band in history. In the ten years they were together, no other group expanded the boundaries of rock and redefined the genre as much as the four cocky lads from Liverpool. No other group so consistently challenged and satisfied their fans. And no other group could ever hope to assemble such an untouchable string of hit singles and imperial albums.

America had been rocked before. Elvis Presley, undisputed king of the genre, was on the charts as early as 1956; Chuck Berry predated him with "Maybelline," which went number five in August 1955. Buddy Holly came next, and the Beach Boys were just beginning to make a splash, but the arrival of the Beatles in America signaled a new era of self-contained rock groups who wrote, recorded, and performed their own material. The ruckus that ensued was staggering. After the Beatles returned to England on February 22,

1964, British bands scrambled to be the next to make the transatlantic journey. By the end of the year, the Rolling Stones, the Dave Clark Five, the Animals, Gerry and the Pacemakers, Herman's Hermits, and the Kinks had all hit U.S. shores and U.S. sales charts. This was the cue for many American kids to buy guitars, form bands, and start their engines.

From the basic yeah-yeah-yeah and three-chord primal stomp of the Beatles' earliest hits to the elaborate orchestrations that turned later compositions into masterpieces, the Fab Four always remained pop-conscious but seemed clairvoyant in detecting the next twist or trend. In the recording studio, they were the first to experiment with feedback ("I Feel Fine" in 1964), distortion ("Revolution" in 1968), and a long line of double-tracking, backwards-masking, and change-of-speed tricks. *Sgt. Pepper's Lonely Hearts Club Band* in June 1967, arguably the greatest rock and roll platter of all time, was one of the first concept albums ever recorded, and it initiated a deeper appreciation of album cover art.

Four distinct personalities who fit together seamlessly at first, they eventually diverged down different paths, and a quicksand of personality clashes sucked them under. Chroniclers of

Above: John Lennon (right) and Paul McCartney (left) led the mop-tops through six songs on the February 9, 1964, telecast of *The Ed Sullivan Show*. Opposite: Pan Am flight 101 from Heathrow, carrying the Fab Four, arrives in New York.

rock have drawn one analogy after another in attempting to explain the perfect Beatles interaction, using everything from a human body (Paul was the heart, John the soul) to a circus (John was the ring-leader, Ringo the clown) to a Chinese smorgasbord (Paul was the sweet baby shrimp in garlic sauce, John the hot-and-sour soup). The four complemented one another so well that divine intervention must have had a hand in their genesis.

John Lennon, born October 9, 1940, in Liverpool, was play-ing in an amateur skiffle group called the Quarrymen the day hewas introduced to Paul McCartney (born June 18, 1942, also in Liverpool) by mutual friend Ivan Vaughan. McCartney could not only play an impressive left-handed guitar, he knew all the words to "Be-Bop-A-Lula," "Twenty-Flight Rock," and a number of

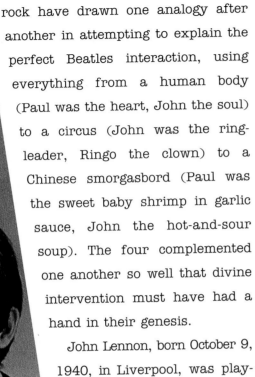

Paul McCartney, the cute Beatle, was born right-handed but at age fourteen he discovered he was more adept on guitar with his left hand on the strings and his right on the fretboard.

other rockabilly and rhythm and blues standards Lennon was eager to learn. In time, the two picked up guitarist George Harrison (born February 25, 1943, in Liverpool) and played under the name Johnny and the Moondogs until they recruited bassist Stu Sutcliffe and drummer Tommy Moore and came up with a new name, the Beatals, which Sutcliffe chose in honor of Buddy Holly's Crickets. The name would soon be changed to the Silver Beetles, and Moore would be replaced by Pete Best in August 1960.

They were loved and revered early on in Hamburg, Germany, where they played Little Richard and Carl Perkins covers at smoky clubs like the Indra and the Kaiserkeller. In January 1961, back home at Liverpool's Cavern Club, they kicked off a string of regular performances that eventually numbered over three hun-dred. When the group returned to Hamburg later that year, Sutcliffe announced his decision to leave the band to pursue his true love, painting. McCartney moved to bass and the band, call-ing itself the Beatles by this point, became a four-piece. (Sutcliffe died of a brain hemorrhage in 1962.)

Twenty-seven-year-old Brian Epstein was running a record-store the day he caught a lunchtime appearance by the Beatles at the Cavern. Within a month, he was their manager and was knocking on every record company door in town trying to land a deal. Every company said no until producer George Martin agreed to cut a few sides for Parlophone records provided the Beatles replace Best, whose style Martin didn't care for. He got no argu-ment from Epstein or the group, and on September 11, 1962, the recast Beatles—with Ringo Starr (born Richard Starkey, Jr., on July 7, 1940, in Liverpool) from fellow Merseyside group Rory Storme and the Hurricanes—cut their first sides for Parlophone, "P.S. I Love You" and "Love Me Do." (Actually, Ringo only shook maracas on the first song and played tambourine on the second. Martin was leery of using Ringo, who had no experience in the stu-dio, and hired seasoned trapsman Andy White to fill the drum stool for this early recording date.)

The single kicked off a six-year stretch of top-twenty U.K. and U.S. hits for the mop-tops, and

Beatlemania began to take flight. When the Beatles reached America, thousands of screaming teenage fans welcomed them at Kennedy Airport and more than seventy million curiosity seekers tuned into *The Ed Sullivan Show* on February 9, 1964, to witness the Beatles' first American television performance.

The music was a bit loud and abrupt for some parents, and the long hair took some getting used to, but in time, the Beatles crossed generational lines and found diverse audiences enjoying "I Want to Hold Your Hand," "She Loves You," "Can't Buy Me Love," "Eight Days a Week," and other hits. Cinema was next. The band starred in two motion pictures directed by Richard Lester, *A Hard Day's Night* (1964) and *Help!* (1965), both critical, as well as commercial, successes. But by 1966, they could no longer play in public without feeling like a parody of themselves. The audiences were too loud and too crazed; the music could barely be heard above the screaming. On August 29, 1966, the Beatles made their last official concert appearance, at San Francisco's Candlestick Park, deciding to concentrate fully on making music in the studio.

Their songs grew more introspective, even political, and Lennon and McCartney became the spokesmen of a generation. Beatles music now meant much more than guitars and drums, and incorporated instruments that other bands were not even think-

From left: George Harrison, Paul McCartney, John Lennon, and Ringo Starr.

ing about toying with. The release of the Beatles' most ambitious work to date, *Sgt. Pepper's Lonely Hearts Club Band*, marked another milestone in rock history. This was rock's first concept album, revolving around a fictional band played by the Fab Four. One of rock's first LPs to open with a gatefold sleeve, it was *the* first to include lyrics. The songs, some examined under a microscope for hidden meanings, flowed from one to another, pausing only a few times. The album inspired a rash of copycats.

The Beatles launched their own label, Apple Records, in early 1968 and later that year released *The Beatles*, called "The White Album" because of its bare, white cover. Now the band's differing tastes became apparent. Paul didn't stray too far from pleasant pop melodies (Lennon accused him of writing "granny music") while John turned to more substantial, which sometimes meant more primal, compositions. Harrison brought in a sitar and songs steeped in Eastern culture. And the presence of Lennon's future wife, avant-garde artist Yoko Ono, added even more spice to the stew. The band grew further apart and their studio sessions for their last two albums, *Abbey Road* (1969) and *Let It Be* (1970), were encumbered by bickering and misery.

In April 1970, McCartney told the press that the band was essentially kaput. When John Lennon was shot and killed on December 8, 1980, all hopes of a proper reunion were dashed, but in 1995 the three surviving Beatles were planning to issue a new version of a Lennon song—with a vocal from Lennon contributed through the magic of technology.

THE ROLLING STONES

While the Beatles wanted to hold your hand, the Rolling Stones couldn't get no satisfaction. They were rock's first bad boys, a bunch of rhythm and blues hellraisers who nicked their sound (as well as their name) from the great blues tradition that spawned howlers Muddy Waters, Jimmy Reed, and Howlin' Wolf. The Stones' defiant—and deviant—image was as potent as their music. They claimed to be the "World's Greatest Rock and Roll Band" and got away with it.

Trouble courted them from the start. The "peeing in public" episode that made headlines in 1964 was kid stuff compared to later nightmares. Riots broke out at Stones concerts as early as 1964, and before the end of the decade, drug busts and fatalities occurred in the band as well as in the audience. But by the seventies, things had cooled down. The Stones staged a glorious comeback in the disco era with *Some Girls* and enjoyed a fruitful second wind. Lippy Mick Jagger was always front and center, but the real star of the Stones show has always been rhythm guitarist Keith Richards. Among rock fans, Richards is usually spoken of in reverent tones. He emerged from the classic rock period surely worse for wear, but as the great survivor of rock and roll nihilism. Not bad for a former choirboy and boy scout.

Boy scout? Yep. Richards joined at age thirteen but was relieved of his cap and scarf two years later, after punching out another recruit. He'd already met Jagger by this point: they had been five-year-old classmates at England's Wentworth Primary School, but fell out of touch until crossing paths again in 1960. The two loved rhythm and blues, and ended up playing together in Little Boy Blue and the Blue Boys. Jagger also sang in Alexis Korner's Blues Incorporated, a blues revival band led by Korner, a virtuoso guitarist who had a huge influence on many of the classic rock shredders. At a Korner gig, Jagger and Richards met Brian Jones, a soft-spoken guitarist and ladies' man (and the father of two illegitimate children by the time he was sixteen) who was also playing with Korner. Jones suggested that he, Jagger, and Richards jam on their own. With Dick Taylor on bass (from the Blue Boys), pianist Ian Stewart, and drummer Mick Avory (later to join the Kinks), the Rolling Stones were born, the name suggested by Jones after a favorite Muddy Waters song. The new troupe played their first gig on July 16, 1962, at the Marquee nightclub in Soho, London.

Jones, Jagger, and Richards shared a flat in Chelsea and were soon pestering the proprietor of the Crawdaddy Club for a Sunday afternoon slot to showcase the Stones' blues appreciation program. Spreading the gospel of Muddy Waters, Bo Diddley, Little Walter, and Chuck Berry, the Stones soon drew turn-away crowds. Avory was eventually replaced by Charlie Watts, a drumming jazz fanatic. Bill Wyman, a family man and air force cadet with a steady job, became the new bassist.

A deal with the Decca label led to their first single, an obscure Berry song, "Come On," backed with Willie Dixon's "I Want to Be Loved." The initial tapes were deemed too raw and unreleasable by Decca, but the redone versions rose to number twenty-two on the British charts. A year later, the Rolling Stones were in America but were met with far less enthusiasm than their Fab Four counterparts. The Stones' take on the blues was a bit too brusque and inaccessible for many ears. At an early multiact show in San Antonio, Texas, the trained monkey on the bill was brought out for encores, but not the Stones. Dean Martin turned them into the butt of jokes when the band made its American television debut on the June 3, 1964, broadcast of *Hollywood Palace*. The dancing elephants that shared the bill went over better.

By the end of 1964, the Stones made the top ten in the U.S. with "Time Is on My Side" and finally made number one the next April with "(I Can't Get No) Satisfaction." Richards had scribbled down the song after waking up from a dream, and thought it nothing but an album filler, but it launched a string of hits—"Get Off My Cloud," "As Tears Go By," "19th Nervous Breakdown," "Paint It Black," "Mother's Little Helper," "Ruby Tuesday"—that didn't let up

The World's Greatest Rock and Roll Band? Guitarists Ron Wood and Keith Richards, singer Mick Jagger, drummer Charlie Watts, and bassist Bill Wyman (from left) would say absolutely. The Rolling Stones, born from the blues in 1962, are still selling out stadiums in the nineties.

until the summer of 1969 with "Honky Tonk Woman" and their last album of the sixties, *Let It Bleed*. It was during the recording of *Let It Bleed* that they lost Brian Jones.

He was found dead at the bottom of his swimming pool on July 3, 1969, just a month after announcing his decision to leave the band. The cause of death was ruled "immersion in fresh water under the influence of drugs and alcohol," and although foul play has always been suspected, it has never been proved.

Enter Mick Taylor, an ex–John Mayall guitarist, who joined the Stones just in time for one of rock's most gruesome moments. As the band was playing on stage at the Altamont Speedway in Livermore, California, a gang of Hell's Angels—hired as a security force—stabbed a spectator to death. The moment was captured in *Gimme Shelter*, a harrowing film documentary of the event, and essentially brought the era of peace, love, and rock festivals to a sad close.

By 1970 the Stones were back with their own label, scoring with the blazin' hot single "Brown Sugar" and the album *Sticky Fingers*. *Exile on Main Street* (1972) was next, but the band showed signs of creative fatigue beginning with *Goat's Head Soup* in 1973. Taylor was out after *It's Only Rock and Roll* (1974), and the Stones

Opposite: In 1975, the Stones settled on guitarist Ron Wood (left, with Jagger) as Mick Taylor's replacement after auditioning scores of session men. (Taylor spent six years with the Stones as Brian Jones' replacement.)

Above left: Keith Richards (right, with Jagger) was a Stone from the start and is still with the band. Above right: Ron Wood (left, with Richards) is likewise still with the band.

snagged Ron Wood from the Faces, who packed it in shortly after Wood split.

In 1978, the Stones refused to be ignored and released their biggest-selling album to date and their last of the decade, *Some Girls*. They easily crossed over to the disco nation and, on the evidence of "Miss You," were suddenly as welcome on the dance floor beneath the mirrored ball as they had been at Madison Square Garden just a few years earlier.

Infrequent album releases continued through the eighties as Jagger and Richards spent the decade sometimes at odds with each other while pursuing solo careers. But the Stones resurface every few years and, in the summer of 1994, they toured again, this time for their album *Voodoo Lounge*.

THE WHO

With an arsenal of jackhammer-strength youth anthems like "My Generation," "Teenage Wasteland," and "The Kids Are Alright," and with acrobatic guitarist Pete Townshend and drummer Keith Moon, the Who attracted more rock fans coming of age in the sixties and seventies than perhaps any other classic rock group.

At a Who show, teenage angst was not only sung about, it was acted out. The band regularly closed their sets by destroying their instruments, often with explosions and a haze of smoke. Now that's entertainment.

They began as the Detours in 1962—with John Entwistle on bass, Pete Townshend on guitar, Dougie Sandon on drums, and Roger Daltrey moving from guitar to the microphone after the original singer split. All were from the London area, and decided to call themselves the Who after they saw another band on television called the Detours. But scene maker and band friend Pete Meadon had another idea, and talked Townshend and his group into aligning the band with the new mod movement and calling themselves the High Numbers, after a term the mods used to convey the epitome of style.

Their sole single, "I'm the Face"/"Zoot Suit," was a flop. Although the mods loved the High Numbers, not many others did, and the band was trapped in mediocrity. Everything changed one evening at a gig at the Royal Oldfield Hotel when loose screw Keith Moon, playing drums at the time in a band called the Beach Combers, declared he could play better than the High Numbers drummer. Townshend and Daltrey let Moon sit in, and he wound up nearly demolishing the kit. Moon played drums like an octopus possessed by demons, and was quite welcome in a band who needed his propulsion.

With their new drummer, the High Numbers went back to being the Who and released their first single, "I Can't Explain," in January 1965. They were virtually ignored by the Brits until they appeared on the *Ready Steady Go!* television program and the nation saw a guitar smashed to bits and a drum kit overturned. The Who were on their way, and from that point, they couldn't finish a gig without destroying their instruments. The crowd (and Moon) demanded it.

In America, it wasn't until 1967 and the release of the "Happy Jack" single that people started to ask, "The who?" The *Happy Jack* album, called *A Quick One* in the U.K., also signaled just where the Who was taking rock and roll. The album's first track, "A Quick One While He's Away," was a nine-minute miniopera that set the stage for future Who epics *Tommy* (1969) and *Quadrophenia* (1973). Tommy, the story of a "deaf, dumb, and blind kid" who becomes a champion pinball player and cult hero, was performed onstage only twice in its entirety—at London's Coliseum in 1969 and New York's Metropolitan Opera House in 1970. *Tommy* was eventually turned into a hit movie starring Daltrey and Ann-Margret in 1975; in 1993, Townshend adapted the story for a Broadway musical.

Solo detours for Townshend, Daltrey, and Moon filled their schedules in the seventies, but the Who did find time to release *The Who By Numbers* (1975) and *Who Are You* (1978) before losing Moon on September 7, 1978, to an overdose of Heminevrin, a sedative prescribed to recovering alcoholics. Kenney Jones, formerly of the Small Faces, sat behind the kit for the next tour, which suffered a tragic blow on December 3, 1979: eleven Who fans were trampled to death in a rush to nab the best seats when only two doors were opened at a general admission concert at Cincinnati's Riverfront Coliseum.

Never a chart-topping singles band—"I Can See for Miles" remains their only top-ten hit—the Who under Townshend's eye were always intent on raising rock and roll to a higher art form. Still, the concert stage was where they generated the most

excitement. Their 1982 tour was called their last, but the Who continued to play various one-offs during the eighties, including the Live Aid benefit concert in 1986. Before the year 2000, they'll most likely be back again.

In the hands of Pete Townshend, a guitar's life was limited. Axe smashing—along with Townshend's windmill arm spins, sky-high leaps, and dramatic leg kicks—became a staple of his performances. Below, circa 1967, Townshend slays; right, he simply plays.

THE DOORS

Even if Jim Morrison had never linked up with the Doors, his poetry might have found an audience on its own. Morrison wrote so many pages of verse that there was enough for two books, excluding the eight albums he wrote with the Doors. His notebooks were stuffed with lines he'd rewrite to perfection; he even offered his poetry to fan magazines and underground newspapers. When he died in 1971, the band set some of the unpublished material to music. Morrison could have limited his vocation to writing, but the world would have been denied one of rock's most dynamic and controversial frontmen.

Morrison's transcendental verses fit perfectly over Ray Manzarek's creepy-crawly organ fills, Robby Krieger's jazzy guitar lines, and John Densmore's tasty, restrained drumming. The Doors' success story hit a high point in its very first chapter: their debut album (*The Doors*) and single ("Light My Fire") both went straight to number one. But their leader was a troubled soul right from the get-go. Morrison's obsession with drugs and his disturbing behavior, both on- and offstage, landed him in hot water with the law on several occasions. (So did twenty-odd paternity suits.)

The Doors' story began on the beach at Venice, California, where Morrison—a Melbourne, Florida, native—and Manzarek, both former UCLA film students, got together one evening in

Far left: Troubled soul Jim Morrison helped the Doors break on through in 1967. Left: Innovative keyboardist Ray Manzarek handled the low notes, as the Doors never had a steady bassist.

1965. Manzarek, who had studied classical piano, was struck by Morrison's poetry, especially a piece Morrison recited for him entitled "Moonlight Drive," and Manzarek suggested they collaborate on songs and form a band. With Krieger and Densmore, both from a group called the Psychedelic Rangers, Morrison christened the band "The Doors" after a line from Aldous Huxley's book about mescaline, *The Doors of Perception*. (The band didn't bother with a bassist; Manzarek handled the low notes on the keyboard.)

At their first gig at L.A.'s London Fog nightclub, the Doors packed the small venue with so many friends that a rousing ovation was inevitable. By the summer of 1966, they were the house band at the Whisky-A-Go-Go, but were asked to leave one evening after debuting "The End," a harrowing epic of more than ten minutes that was spoke-sung by Morrison, in which a young boy wants to murder his parents. The song shocked the Whisky management, who promptly cut short the Doors' four-month run.

The Doors was released in 1967 and, on the strength of "Light My Fire," reached the top of the charts. Their third album, *Waiting for the Sun* (1968), included their second top-ten single, "Hello, I Love You," the only Doors song ever to use a bass player. (Ray Davies of the Kinks thought the song was too similar to his "All Day and All of the Night" and sued the Doors. The Kinks received all U.K. royalties.) That album also introduced "The Lizard King," a character/alter ego/pen name dreamed up by Morrison for his "The Celebration of the Lizard King," a poem printed inside the record jacket. A portion of the

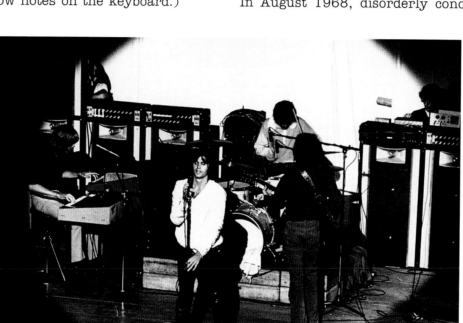

Morrison's public drunkenness marred more than one concert appearance. In New Haven, cops stormed the stage after Morrison mumbled to the crowd that he and a girl had been maced by police in his dressing room.

piece became the lyrics for "Not to Touch the Earth," and the entire "Celebration" ended up on *Absolutely Live* two years later. The *Soft Parade* album (1969) included horns and strings and the band's third top-ten single, "Touch Me."

As the Doors catalog of songs grew, so did Morrison's rap sheet. In December 1967, he was arrested for public obscenity during a New Haven concert. (The police rushed the stage.) In August 1968, disorderly conduct aboard an airplane landed him in handcuffs, and on March 1, 1969, Morrison bottomed out. During a concert at Miami's Dinner Key Auditorium, he broke down in the middle of a song, apparently drunk out of his mind, and, by some accounts, screamed to the crowd, "You wanna see my cock?" Before the audience had a chance to reply, Morrison allegedly unzipped.... The Lizard King was charged with lewd and lascivious behavior, though he was never convicted, and all Doors concerts for the next five months were canceled.

After recording *L.A. Woman* in 1970, Morrison left the Doors for a life in Paris with his wife, Pamela, but died under mysterious circumstances the following year. Official records state that he was found dead in his bathtub on July 3, 1971, the victim of a heart attack, but few saw the corpse. One who did was Pamela, who died of a heroin overdose just three years later. By that time, Morrison's grave at Père Lachaise cemetery in Paris had become a mecca for fans and tourists, who, to this day, scrawl graffiti over Morrison's gravestone as well as those of neighboring plots.

CLASSIC ROCK

JIMI HENDRIX

Jimi Hendrix was the king of all classic rock guitarists. He threw out the rule book and redefined what the electric ax could accomplish. Feedback, neck-tapping, sustained harmonics, whammy-bar and fuzz-box embellishments—Jimi popularized them all and served as the inspiration for the many guitarists who followed. His music has never grown outdated. Even into the nineties, Hendrix compilations continue to pop up on record store shelves. Jimi was the original Seattle rocker, and his legend just keeps growing.

No one played like Hendrix; even his traditional setup was unique. He was a lefty, but always flipped and restrung right-handed guitars. This put the control knobs at the top, which he favored. (Quality left-handed guitars were hard to come by in his heyday.)

Born John Allen Hendrix on November 27, 1942 (his father changed his son's name to James Marshall Hendrix at age four), he was a shy kid. He could never read music, and taught himself to play by listening to records by Muddy Waters, B.B. King, Chuck Berry, and Eddie Cochran for hours on end. Hendrix honed his chops in high school bands and entered the military at age seventeen as a paratrooper in the 101st Airborne Division. Following his honorable discharge after a parachuting accident, he found pickup work backing soul and rhythm and blues greats B.B. King, Sam Cooke, the Isley Brothers, Jackie Wilson, and Little Richard. By 1964, he was in New York playing Greenwich Village nightclubs as Jimmy James and the Blue Flames.

Former Animals bassist Chas Chandler caught a Blue Flames gig at the Cafe Wha?, was absolutely floored, and talked Jimi into flying back to London with him. There Chandler and Hendrix assembled the Jimi Hendrix Experience with Noel Redding on bass and former British television child star John "Mitch" Mitchell on drums. Hendrix burst onto the London music scene without the slightest warning and was immediately the talk of the town. No one had ever seen a guitarist play with such a mix of emotion and abandon. Psychedelia and flower power were just beginning to

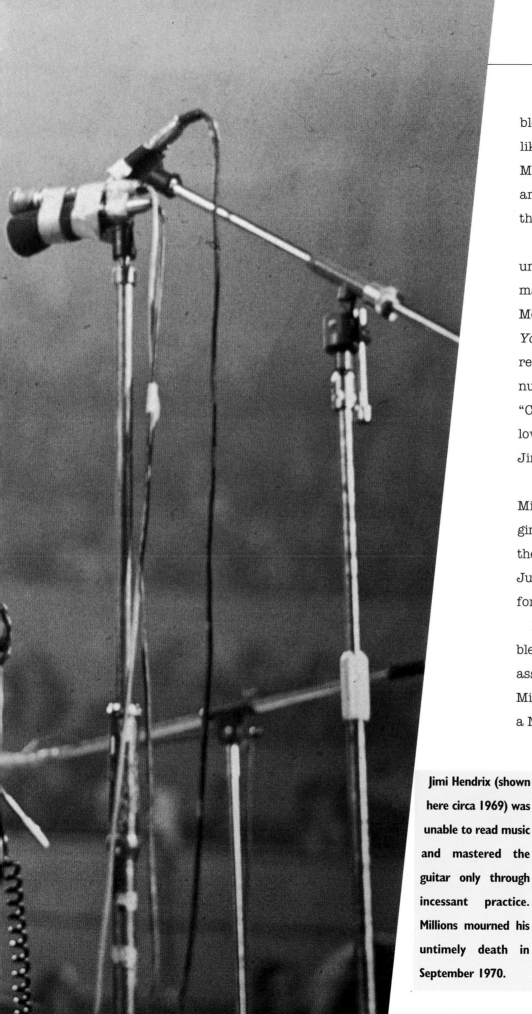

blossom, and Jimi was the ideal symbol of the times. He played like a wild man, exceeding all limits of sixties decency. Paul McCartney, John Lennon, Eric Clapton, Jeff Beck, Brian Jones, and others who caught those early London club gigs had to pick up their jaws from the floor after Hendrix left the stage.

America didn't get a glimpse of the Jimi Hendrix Experience until June 1967, when the band delivered an incendiary performance (at the finale, Hendrix lit his Stratocaster on fire) at the Monterey Pop Festival. Sales of the Experience's debut album, *Are You Experienced?*, took off and by 1968 Hendrix was so hot he released two albums, *Axis: Bold As Love* and *Electric Ladyland* (a number one best-seller). "Purple Haze," "Fire," "Little Wing," and "Crosstown Traffic" all blared from FM radio speakers. Hendrix loved Bob Dylan, too, and "All Along the Watchtower" became Jimi's classic Dylan cover.

By 1969, Jimi's behavior was growing too erratic for Redding and Mitchell to deal with. If Hendrix didn't think the audience was digging a show, he'd walk off midset. He was consuming drugs around the clock and cavorting with any groupie who propositioned him. On July 1, 1969, the Jimi Hendrix Experience played their final performance, at the Denver Pop Festival.

For the Woodstock Festival, Hendrix played with a large ensemble calling themselves the Electric Sky Church. Later that year, he assembled the Band of Gypsys (with Billy Cox on bass and Buddy Miles on drums), who would play only two shows live. Their debut, a New Year's Day gig at New York's Fillmore East, was recorded and released as *Band of Gypsys*. Their second show, at Madison Square Garden, was an out-and-out disaster. During the second song, Hendrix unstrapped his guitar, told the full house, "I'm sorry, we just can't get it together," and left the stage.

Hendrix re-formed the Experience with Cox and Mitchell and turned in a successful U.S. tour in 1970, but on September 18 of that year, it was all over. When he wouldn't rouse from his sleep, his girlfriend, Monika Danneman, called for an ambulance. Hendrix was rushed to St. Mary's Abbot Hospital, where he died at 11:25 A.M. The cause of death was listed as "inhalation of vomit due to barbiturate intoxication."

Jimi Hendrix (shown here circa 1969) was unable to read music and mastered the guitar only through incessant practice. Millions mourned his untimely death in September 1970.

PINK FLOYD

There wasn't a classic rock band more out there than Pink Floyd. They have sold an astonishing number of records—more than 140 million worldwide—while somehow remaining the flip-side of "commercial."

Songs encompass entire album sides, with mood pieces their forte. Insanity was often at the core of their lyrical themes. And at times, the music could hardly be called rock and roll. Tape loops, sound effects, electronic blips from outer space, and orchestral passages pervaded their records. Later, elaborate setups like giant balloons and thirty-foot (9.1m) -high walls turned their arena concerts into the epitome of the art-rock experience.

Mason in 1965, they became a jazz-rock group, the Architectural Abdabs. Barrett, a former student of London's Camberwell School of Art, was already dropping acid in 1965, and his experiments with noise and feedback led to Close's departure and a new name, the Pink Floyd Sound.

At early London nightclub dates, the Pink Floyd Sound filled the space between rock standards like "Louie Louie" and "Roadrunner" with psychedelic excursions. "Arnold Layne" and "See Emily Play," bizarre bursts of delightful psychedelic pop, were their first British singles, which led to their album debut in 1967, *The Pipers at the Gates of Dawn*.

A record deal with EMI-Capitol meant numerous promotional appearances, television guest spots, and playing the corporate game, which Barrett would have no part of. On Dick Clark's *American Bandstand* the band was required to lip-sync, but when the camera zoomed in on Barrett, his mouth was sealed shut. (A friend later explained, "Syd wasn't moving his lips that day.") On *The Pat Boone Show*, Barrett countered the host's questions with a blank stare. After picking up guitarist David Gilmour in time for their second album, *A Saucerful of Secrets* (1968), Barrett left the band to check into a psychiatric hospital, then secluded himself in his mother's house before releasing a few solo albums.

Bassist/singer Roger Waters (left) and guitarist/singer Syd Barrett (above). It was Barrett who dreamed up the name the Pink Floyd Sound, derived from Georgia bluesmen Pink Anderson and Floyd Council.

Syd Barrett is the knight errant to thank. When he teamed with bassist Roger Waters, guitarist Bob Close, keyboardist Rick Wright, and drummer Nick

Even with Barrett out of the picture, Floyd continued their full-speed progressive course. *The Atom Heart Mother* (1970) and *Meddle* (1971) albums both featured side-long epics. The tours became more adventurous as well. A ten-piece orchestra and twenty-member choir accompanied Floyd on the *Atom Heart Mother* tour.

In 1973 came the release of *Dark Side of the Moon*. Now the weirdness was packaged in a strong set of songs, most notably "Time" and "Money," and it turned the members of Pink Floyd into certified rock stars. The album stayed on the *Billboard* magazine charts until 1988—an astounding fifteen-year run, never to be duplicated. You couldn't call Floyd acid rock anymore.

Wish You Were Here (1975), *Animals* (1977), and *The Wall* (1979) went multiplatinum as well, and Pink Floyd concerts became expensive multimedia spectacles. A giant jet balloon crashed onto the stage during the *Dark Side* and *Wish* shows.

Pink Floyd (from left: Nick Mason, Syd Barrett, Roger Waters, and Rick Wright) pioneered the slide and light shows that later became fixtures of rock concert culture.

Inflated pigs flew over stadiums for *Animals*. For the *Wall* tour, a giant wall was constructed during the show, block by Styrofoam block, until the band was obscured. *The Wall* also yielded Floyd's sole number one single, "Another Brick in the Wall (Part II)."

In 1981, tension within the group led to Wright's departure, and the three remaining members recorded *The Final Cut* in 1983. The album was dismally received compared with their million-sellers, and Pink Floyd split up. A few years later, Gilmour, Mason, and Wright resurrected the Pink Floyd name for the album *A Momentary Lapse of Reason*. This infuriated Waters, who preferred that the name rest in peace. In 1986, he filed a lawsuit against Gilmour and Mason, and both parties traded nasty accusations in the rock press. Pink Floyd, the band that spent the late seventies building a wall on arena concert stages, closed out the eighties in law offices, trying to break down an even bigger wall.

LED ZEPPELIN

Led Zeppelin didn't crash-land until 1980, but turn on any classic rock radio station and before the hour's up they'll be "getting the Led out!" Zeppelin fathered heavy metal, and spawned enough imitators to fill every seat in Madison Square Garden. Unfortunately, only a handful of those counterfeiters have matched Zep's dynamics and complexity.

As heavy as they were, many Zeppelin songs used acoustic guitars. Ex-Yardbird Jimmy Page, Zep's lead guitarist and visionary, experimented in the studio as no other producer did: he miked John Paul Jones' bass and John Bonham's drums to maximum volume; toyed with echo, distortion, feedback, and reverb; and laid tasty lick after crunchy riff next to Robert Plant's custom high-pitched vocals.

After the Yardbirds disbanded in 1968, Page hooked up with Plant, who brought in Bonham from his old Birmingham group, Band of Joy. With Jones, an old mate of Page's, they joined forces one evening in a London basement and blew apart the floorboards with a tryout version of "Train Kept A'Rollin'" from the Yardbirds' repertoire. They toured briefly as the New Yardbirds until settling on Led Zeppelin after Who drummer Keith Moon allegedly joked that Page's new band would go over "like a lead zeppelin."

Above: Led Zeppelin's John Paul Jones, Jimmy Page, and Robert Plant (from left) called it a day after drummer John Bonham died in September 1980. Plant (opposite) continued to perform, both solo and, in 1994, again with Page.

Moon wasn't the only one to throw daggers at Page's new outfit. *Rolling Stone* magazine's review of their debut album, *Led Zeppelin* (1969), suggested that they "find a producer, editor, and some material worthy of their collective talents." *Led Zeppelin II* rocked harder. The band disdained singles, but "Whole Lotta Love" climbed all the way to number four on *Billboard*'s chart. (While Zep's signature tune, "Stairway to Heaven," was never commercially released as a single, it remains the most-broadcast rock song of all time.)

Concert profits grew and hotel rooms where Zeppelin stayed got trashed as the band released *Led Zeppelin III* (1970), the untitled fourth album in 1971 (which included "Stairway to Heaven" and was called *Led Zeppelin IV* or *Zoso* by fans), *Houses of the Holy*

(1974), and *Physical Graffiti* (1975). At one point in 1975, all six Zep albums charted simultaneously, another classic rock milestone. Zeppelin was the biggest band in the land. On Dick Cavett's late-night television show, President Gerald Ford's daughters told the host that Zep was their favorite group.

Lady Bad Luck hit next with a string of troubles. In August 1975, Plant totaled his car, seriously injuring himself and putting a hiatus on touring for a period. After the release of *Presence* and the movie and soundtrack double-album for *The Song Remains the Same*, both in 1976, a case of tonsillitis sidelined Plant again. Then, at a Cincinnati show, one hundred Zeppelinites were arrested after crashing the gates. Bonham was busted in Oakland, after allegedly assaulting a member of concert promoter Bill Graham's staff. And in July 1977, Plant's six-year-old son, Karac, died of a respiratory ailment, sadly bringing another tour to an abrupt end.

Zeppelin bounced back in 1979 with *In Through the Out Door*, which held the number one slot for seven weeks. But the mother of all bad news came next. On September 25, 1980, Bonham choked to death on his own vomit after downing forty shots of vodka. He was only thirty-two. Without "Bonzo," Page and Plant put Led Zeppelin to rest for other pursuits. Although the band reunited a few times in the eighties with fill-in drummers (and in 1994 with Bonham's son Jason on drums, but minus Jones), Plant has often said he prefers that Led Zeppelin remain an entity of the past.

CHAPTER TWO

THE BRITISH INVASION

From England they came, in narrow neckties, natty dinner jackets, and pressed trousers, with pudding-bowl haircuts, a vast appreciation of blues standards, and their minds made up to continue the commotion started in 1964 by the Beatles. Consider pre-invasion America. The top pop singles of 1963 were lighthearted balls of fluff: "Hey Paula" by Paul and Paula, "I Will Follow Him" by Little Peggy March, "It's My Party" by Leslie Gore, and so on. Two of the best-selling books of that year, *Happiness Is a Warm Puppy* and *Security Is a Thumb and a Blanket*, were penned by Charles Schultz of the Peanuts comic strip. Television viewers couldn't get enough of *The Beverly Hillbillies*, *Candid Camera*, and *Bonanza*. Everything was so white-bread, so polite. But that fragile scene was about to shatter.

With the assassination of President John Kennedy in November 1963, the youth of America needed new heroes. They had tried out the values Kennedy extolled—patriotism, order peace, fair play—and had seen their champion literally shot down. In a world that could erupt in chaos at any moment, perhaps it was best to embrace the chaos. America's kids wanted to rock, and Pat Boone's watered-down versions of Fats Domino and Little Richard songs just weren't cutting it anymore: Britain's bad boys stepped into the breach.

Keith Relf of the Yardbirds; Jeff Beck; the Animals' Eric Burdon.

CLASSIC ROCK

Liberation was in the air, especially within the black community. Dr. Martin Luther King, Jr., led 200,000 demonstrators down Constitution Avenue in Washington, D.C., and delivered his uplifting "I have a dream" speech in August 1963, just two months after three African-Americans had registered at the University of Alabama despite Governor George Wallace's threats to maintain racial segregation. The times they were a-changin' and the British bands, already rocking their native country with blues rave-ups, knew that American kids were itching to pick up the beat. The Beatles had proven that. Some of the acts were clean-cut ladies and gentlemen even Mom could appreciate: the Searchers, Gerry and the Pacemakers, Dusty Springfield, Freddie and the Dreamers. Some were a little rougher: Herman's Hermits, the Dave Clark Five, the Swingin' Blue Jeans. Then there were the bands who have stood the test of time and still get plenty of airplay on classic rock radio. They are the subject of this chapter.

After the blues revivalists of 1964, the U.S. welcomed another crop of Brits later in the decade. This lot rocked harder, their songs were longer and louder, and their look was even shabbier. America greeted both movements with open arms.

THE FIRST INVASION
THE ANIMALS

With more rhythm and blues in their blood than any of their fellow British rockers, the Animals stormed America in 1964 on the strength of the ominous "House of the Rising Sun," their second single.

The scruffy Eric Burdon could belt 'em out with the best of the rhythm-and-blues artists of the day, but Burdon wasn't the band's first leader. Keyboardist Alan Price initially formed the group in the late fifties as the Alan Price Combo, a jazz trio with bassist Chas Chandler and drummer John Steele. Guitarist Hilton Valentine eventually signed on, followed by Burdon, whose presence shifted the band toward rhythm and blues. With Price no longer the singer or centerpiece, the group altered its name to the Kansas City Five, but the Saturday night crowd at the Downbeat Club in Newcastle-on-Tyne insisted on calling them "the Animals" because of the

Eric Burdon (right) took the Animals straight to number one with "House of the Rising Sun."

band's shabby clothes and Burdon's wild manner.

Bob Dylan's 1962 debut album included versions of two songs that would become the Animals' first two singles. Their first slice o' wax, a snappy reworking of the traditional folk song "Baby, Let Me Follow You Down," was updated to "Baby Let Me Take You Home" and shifted into raucous double-time for the final verse and coda. In England, they toured with Chuck Berry, became regulars at London's Scene Club, and then recorded a four-and-a-half-minute version (considered overly long for the day) of "House of the Rising Sun."

The single topped the charts in England and America, paving the way for a transatlantic flight to the States. A cover version of Nina Simone's "Don't Let Me Be Misunderstood" made the top twenty, and the Animals' strongest follow-ups were "We Gotta Get Out of This Place" and "It's My Life," both penned by Tin Pan Alley songsmiths. Their albums, meanwhile, were studded with rhythm and blues standards. Their repertoire even overlapped the Stones' with gritty versions of "Around and Around" and "She Said Yeah."

The dissension that hounded the band from its first days together came to a head in 1965, and Price announced his departure. He cited "fear of flying" as the official reason, but it might have been the turmoil brought on by Burdon's alleged LSD use. From May 1965 until the end of 1966, Burdon lost his bandmates one by one until he was left with a crew of nobodies, albeit with the new moniker he had long craved: Eric Burdon and the Animals. The revamped Animals hit with "See See Rider" in 1966 and "San Franciscan Nights" in 1967 before throwing in the towel in July 1968.

Burdon recorded with War, and had a number three hit in 1970 with "Spill the Wine." The Animals re-formed in December 1968 for a one-shot concert, again in 1977 for a comeback album, *Before We Were So Rudely Interrupted*, and in 1983 for the poorly received *Ark* and an equally dismal greatest-hits live album.

THE HOLLIES

Next to the Beatles, no other British band churned out as many cheerful and carefree singles in their native country as the Hollies. And they nearly duplicated their U.K. success in the U.S., hitting first with "Look Through Any Window" in 1966, and continuing with "Bus Stop," "Stop Stop Stop," and "Carrie Anne," the last three top ten hits. After Graham Nash left in 1968, the Hollies scored again with "He Ain't Heavy, He's My Brother" and a future classic rock staple, "Long Cool Woman (in a Black Dress)" (1972), before turning toward the soft rock of "The Air That I Breathe" in 1974.

Singer Allan Clarke formed the band with Nash, a childhood friend from Manchester. Known first as the Deltas with bassist Eric

The Hollies mixed lilting melodies and warm harmonies with more distinction than any of their British counterparts.

Haydock and drummer Donald Rathbone, then the Dominators of Rhythm, they settled on the name the Hollies—as a tribute to Buddy Holly—when guitarist Tony Hicks joined. Like many of their counterparts, the Hollies concentrated on American rhythm and blues standards before scoring their first U.K. hit with "Just One Look" (1964). Americans didn't catch on until two years later.

When the band foolishly decided to record an album of Bob Dylan covers (those songs had worked for the Byrds and the Animals), Nash saw trouble coming and left to form Crosby, Stills and Nash. Terry Sylvester of the Swingin' Blue Jeans replaced Nash; the Dylan tribute bombed, Clarke left, then rejoined; and the Hollies continued to record into the eighties.

THE KINKS

The Kinks deserve the award for longevity. Only a handful of groups has lasted as long—more than thirty years—as the mod-tops from Muswell Hill, England. And their first hit single, "You Really Got Me" (1964), with its raunchy, fat-lick guitar intro, is often cited as the early blueprint for many of the heavy-metal songs that followed.

Ray Davies and his younger brother Dave, the youngest of eight children, learned to play instruments early on, just as their siblings had. By age nine, Ray owned a Spanish guitar and was developing an interest in the blues. By seventeen, he was studying at Hornsey Art College and playing nights with the Dave Hunt Band, a jazz outfit, until he joined brother Dave's band, the Ravens.

Robert Wace, the Ravens' original singer, often had a difficult time winning over the crowd at the ritzy dance halls they played. Legend has it that one evening the boos and airborne beverages in the direction of Wace's face proved too much, and Wace turned to his rhythm guitarist, Ray, and shouted, "You'll have to sing now!" Ray became the singer, and Wace opted to serve as the Ravens' comanager.

After changing their name to the Kinks, the Davies brothers, with the Ravens' bassist Pete Quaife and drummer Mick Avory, recorded their first single, a cover of Little Richard's "Long Tall Sally," which sounded nearly identical to the Beatles version. It went nowhere, as did a follow-up, "You Still Want Me," a Ray Davies original.

Dave Davies was not a stellar guitarist in those days, so he experimented with sounds using his too-small amplifier to make up for his shortcomings. One day he ripped the amp apart, connected its speakers to a bigger Vox amplifier, and voila! He created rock's first fuzzbox. A version of a new Ray original, "You Really Got Me," was

How did they become the Kinks? According to Ray Davies, one day he arrived at the recording studio dressed in a garish orange tie and someone remarked, "Now you really look like a kink." The name stuck.

recorded with the new contraption, as was a cleaner, more polite version. But the loud take was the one that made it to record shops and to number seven on the American singles charts. It may have been a loose rewrite of the Kingsmen's 1963 hit, "Louie Louie," but the Kinks followed it up with the equally impressive "All Day and All of the Night" and "Tired of Waiting for You," both in 1965. In England, the Kinks' popularity rivaled even the biggest bands of the day. (In America, those early Kinks singles actually charted higher than the Stones' first hits.)

By the mid-sixties, Ray Davies was a songsmith in demand, penning tunes for the Animals, the Seekers, and even Peggy Lee. His writing took a turn toward social satire on Kinks hits "A Well Respected Man" and "Dedicated Follower of Fashion." But the band hit a dry spell after the release of "Sunny Afternoon" in 1966. Then concept-album fever struck the Davies brothers. Albums like *The Kinks Are the Village Green Preservation Society* and *Arthur, or the Decline and Fall of the British Empire,* both from 1969, were well received by critics, but did little to advance the Kinks' career. A union battle stemming from a *Hullabaloo* television show appearance banned them from performing in the States again until 1969. They returned with a vengeance in 1970 with "Lola," who "walked like a woman and talked like a man."

The Kinks underwent several personnel changes through the seventies, but Ray and Dave always stayed at the helm, even as messy fraternal arguments interrupted their concerts. (Or were the fights part of the show?) They hit the singles charts again in 1978 with "A Rock 'N' Roll Fantasy" and in 1983 with "Come Dancing." Revitalized by the New Wave scene, they packed arenas with new and old fans alike.

MANFRED MANN

Manfred Mann's career, like that of the Moody Blues, can be easily divided into two distinct parts. There were early triumphs, like "Do Wah Diddy Diddy" (1964) and "Mighty Quinn (Quinn the Eskimo)" (1968), a Dylan cover. But Mann returned in the mid-seventies, assembled the Earth Band, and caused quite a stir with two Bruce Springsteen songs.

Born Michael Lubowitz in South Africa, Mann was a fixture on the British music scene as early as 1962, when he formed the Mann-Hugg Blues Brothers with Mike Hugg. In the early days Mann's horn-rimmed glasses and Abe Lincoln beard stood out in any crowd, but his keyboard playing paled in comparison to his contemporaries. Renaming themselves Manfred Mann, with singer Paul Jones at the fore, the group's big break came when their third single, "5-4-3-2-1," became the signature tune for the popular British television show *Ready Steady Go!* Their first chart success, "Do Wah Diddy Diddy," went all the way to number one in the States in 1964. "Sha La La" went top twenty later that year, and the Manfreds struck again with "Pretty Flamingo" (1966). A love affair with Dylan's songwriting led to the top-ten success of "Mighty Quinn" in 1968.

In June 1969, the band said so long to singles in favor of an ill-advised career in jazz-rock fusion. As fusionists, they were practically laughed out of town and didn't resurface until years later, when Mann formed his new Manfred Mann's Earth Band with singer Mick Rogers. With heavier, synthesizer-driven music, Mann toured endlessly in the States. A version of Bruce Springsteen's "Blinded by the Light," released in 1976, returned the

Manfred Mann took "Mighty Quinn" into the top ten in 1968, but it was take another eight years before he hit the charts again. This time he scored with the Bruce Springsteen song "Blinded by the Light."

Manfreds to the top spot in America. Mann recognized a huge songwriting talent in Springsteen, similar to that of Dylan, so another Springsteen song was recorded and released. But "Spirit in the Night" (1977) was only a minor hit for Mann. Springsteen, a Manfred Mann fan himself, returned the favor by adding "Pink Flamingo" to his concert repertoire, though he never recorded the song.

THE YARDBIRDS

Yes, Virginia, there really was a rock band in the sixties that served as the springboard for not one but three future guitar heroes. Six-string gurus Jeff Beck, Eric Clapton, and Jimmy Page all perfected their ax pyrotechnics in the seminal blues-based rock outfit the Yardbirds, and all went on to greater successes.

Of that mighty triumvirate, Clapton was the first to become a Yardbird. He was asked to join the band to replace original guitarist Anthony "Top" Topham. In the summer of 1963, the career of the Yardbirds, in residency at London's Marquee nightclub and Richmond's Crawdaddy Club, was beginning to soar. But come September, Top's parents would have none of it and forced him to continue his schooling. His guitar was stored away, as was his tenure with the Yardbirds.

Clapton, fresh from stints with the Roosters and Casey Jones and the Engineers, joined a motley bunch that already included fellow guitarist Chris Dreja, howler Keith Relf, bassist Paul Samwell-Smith, and drummer Jim McCarty. Extensive touring led to a recording contract with EMI in spring 1964. "I Wish You Would" was their first single in the U.K., mistakenly released as "I Wish You Could" in the U.S. in August 1964.

After package tours with the Kinks and one-shot concert dates with the Beatles, Clapton began to grow tired of the band. When it was decided to record a song called "For Your Love" by a totally unknown Manchester songwriter named Graham Gouldman (future bassist for the band 10cc), Clapton balked. He finally agreed to play on it, but only the middle-eight portion, and flew from the Yardbirds before the record's release in March 1965. The single became the band's first hit in the States and their biggest ever. "For Your Love" went all the way to number six on the *Billboard* magazine singles chart. The song also served as the title track of their first American album, a compilation of previous singles, released in June 1965 on the Epic label.

Who could replace Clapton? First, an up-and-coming session guitarist, Jimmy Page, was asked aboard. But Page was content with studio work, and suggested that the one-hit Yardbirds recruit the guitarist from the Tridents, his friend Jeff Beck.

Beck's flashy guitarplay took the Yardbirds to greater heights. His experiments with feedback and distortion led them increasingly away from the blues and into uncharted psychedelic territory, and when they embarked on their first American tour in 1965, all eyes and ears were on Beck and his incredible solos. Successful singles and albums with the virtuoso followed, most notably "I'm a Man" in November 1965.

By early 1966, bassist Samwell-Smith was exhausted and flew the coop for a full-time career in production. Enter Page, who played bass for a spell but in due time strapped on a six-string. During a concert in Phoenix, Beck snapped, pushing an amp out the window of an overcrowded nightclub. Two weeks later, he broke down in Kansas City and told the band he couldn't continue. Dreja moved to bass and Page became the lead guitarist. Once in a while, however, Beck would join in. The single "Happenings Ten Years Time Ago," backed with the brief "Psycho Daisies," is Beck and Page's only recorded studio appearance together with the Yardbirds (John Paul Jones played bass), except for a brief scene in the movie *Blow-Up*. Beck did eventually join for a package tour with the Stones and Ike and Tina Turner. Guitar enthusiasts today drool at the thought of the Beck/Page lineup.

Beck left for good in late 1966, and although the lineup soldiered on with Page, the band was history by 1968. With drummer John Bonham and singer Robert Plant, Page formed the New Yardbirds, which would later evolve into Led Zeppelin.

THE ZOMBIES

There was nothing spooky about the Zombies, a mis-named rock band if ever there was one. But the brief career of these clean-cuts was full of odd twists and turns, not to mention three of the most delightful pop songs of all time, "She's Not There," "Tell Her No," and "Time of the Season." No other rock band con-centrated as much on minor-key compositions as this five-piece band from Herts. Theirs was a worldwide success story, but they were never adored in their native England as much they were in America.

Keyboardist Rod Argent and lead guitarist Paul Atkinson were honor students at St. Albans school before teaming up with drummer Hugh Grundy, singer Colin Blunstone, and bassist Chris White to jam in White's father's shop. Original bassist Paul Arnold had been sacked after attempting to play "Peggy Sue" with one hand in his pocket.

A recording contract with the Decca label (Parrot in the States) led to the first single, "She's Not There" (1964), which the Zombies nailed in one take. Argent's electric piano was a fresh departure from the guitar-driven records of the day, and the debut was an inter-national hit, climbing all the way to number two in the U.S. Their next hit in the States, "Tell Her No" (1965), holds the distinction of being the most negative song in history. The word "no" is repeated seventy times.

"Time of the Season," their third and final hit in America, was originally released on their well-received 1967 album *Odyssey and Oracle*, but it wasn't until February 1969 that the single hit number two in the U.S. The Zombies had already disbanded by this point, with no intention of re-forming, but a shady promoter took it upon himself to package together a group of no-names and send them out on the road as the Zombies.

The fake Zombies, naturally, looked nothing like the originals, and when the press questioned their authenticity, the phonies responded with a whopper: the original singer had been killed in a car crash and it was his last wish that the group continue! Litigation from Argent and company put an end to the charade, but not before the fake Zombies toured with an equally fake Animals.

Colin Blunstone enjoyed a modest solo career into the eighties. Rod Argent formed the band Argent in 1969 and reached the top five in 1972 with "Hold Your Head Up."

A group of lads who called themselves the Zombies took "She's Not There," their first single, to number two in the U.S. There was certainly nothing eerie about this group of gentlemen, led by singer Colin Blunstone (left).

CLASSIC ROCK

THE SECOND INVASION
BADFINGER

Through their association with the Beatles, Badfinger should have had it made. But they rarely caught a break, and star status always eluded them. They ended in misery and sorely in debt.

Singer/guitarist Pete Ham and drummer Mike Gibbons had been in the Iveys—one of the first bands to sign with the Beatles' Apple label—since 1966. Paul McCartney didn't care for their demos, but John Lennon and George Harrison expressed enthusiasm and took the band under their wing. "Maybe Tomorrow," their first single, reached number sixty in the States but went nowhere in the U.K. In fact, no one was happy being in or associated with the Iveys. Perhaps a name change was in order.

McCartney suggested they use "Home." Lennon favored "Prix." Apple Records executive Neil Aspinall won out with "Badfinger," and the newly christened band began work on the soundtrack for *The Magic Christian*, a film starring Ringo Starr and Peter Sellers. Included was the McCartney-penned "Come and Get It," Badfinger's first single in the

Badfinger's original name, the Iveys, was intentionally derivative of the Hollies, whose sound they copied as well.

States and a top-ten hit. An all-originals album, *No Dice* (produced by Beatles engineer Geoff Emerick), yielded their second U.S. hit, "No Matter What."

Badfinger members played on the sessions for Lennon's *Imagine* album, Ringo Starr's hit "It Don't Come Easy," and Harrison's *All Things Must Pass*, which led Harrison to invite Badfinger to join him for the Concert for Bangladesh held at New York City's Madison Square Garden on August 1, 1971.

Their third album, *Straight Up*, produced by Harrison and Todd Rundgren, included Badfinger's final two singles, "Day After Day" and "Baby Blue." Even though a million copies of "Day After Day" were sold, a bum contract deal continued to plague the group with financial woes. Rundgren had more or less been forced upon them, and according to the band, he had no respect for their ideas.

Two albums for the Warners Bros. label failed to break the top one hundred, and the record company ended up suing the band when the band's advance money couldn't be found in an escrow account. And things only got worse for Badfinger: on April 23, 1975, Pete Ham was found dead in his garage/studio. He had hanged himself, leaving behind a note cursing the music industry.

THE JEFF BECK GROUP

In 1966, the Yardbirds were touring America with Gary Lewis and the Playboys and singer/songwriter Bobby Hebb as part of Dick Clark's Caravan Tour when Beck announced he had had enough. He returned to England with aspirations of putting together his own band, a group that would truly showcase his unique and evolving guitarplay. On his later recordings and appearances with the Yardbirds, Beck had become a more experimental showman. His playing was still rooted in the blues, but now his solos were spinning off into new and uncharted directions toward jazz, fusion, and psychedelia.

After attempting several different lineups, Beck finally settled on drummer Mick Waller, bassist Ron Wood (who started on guitar but switched to bass after Beck was disappointed with his original choice), and an upstart singer named Rod Stewart, who was from Long John Baldry's band, Steampacket. Calling themselves the Jeff Beck Group, they recorded *Truth* in 1968, a landmark album that featured Beck's incandescent solos front and center next to Stewart's sandpaper vocals. Heavy metal might have been born on this disc.

After a blistering performance at New York City's Fillmore East concert hall ("Beck Upstages Grateful Dead!" blared the *New York Times* headline), the band followed up with a year-long tour

The Jeff Beck Group (from left: Rod Stewart, Ron Wood, Mick Waller, and Beck) is among those credited with the birth of heavy metal, on their *Truth* LP, recorded in London in 1968.

and then the equally raucous *Beck-Ola* in 1969. No one had ever heard "Jailhouse Rock" and "All Shook Up" played quite this heavy before, and after the record's release, they never would again. Inflated egos tore the band apart. The Jeff Beck Group, advertised to appear at the Woodstock festival in August, pulled out at the last minute. Beck, with frazzled nerves and no control over the sound system, figured the group was doomed to fail. The Jeff Beck Group split up.

But Beck knew that Stewart was too good to lose, so he asked the singer to join a new group that would include ex–Vanilla Fudge's Tim Bogert on bass and Carmine Appice on drums. Stewart declined, preferring to record solo and follow Ron Wood into the Faces. A horrible car crash in November 1969 put Beck's career on hold for more than a year.

He finally recruited and recorded with an all-new Jeff Beck Group, with singer Bob Tench replacing Stewart, but that lineup never matched the power of the first group. Nor did Beck, Bogart, and Appice, who overplayed everything they got their hands on. Canning vocals altogether for *Blow by Blow* (1975), an all-instrumental excursion, was a wise move. This jazz-fusion record still stands as his best recording.

BLIND FAITH

They lasted only a year, toured once, and released just one album, but what an album it was. *Blind Faith* (1969) was a classic rock masterpiece, and marked the birth of rock's first supergroup. Its controversial cover also afforded many American teenage boys their first glimpse at a pair of breasts.

Guitarist Eric Clapton and drummer Ginger Baker had made a name for themselves in Cream. Steve Winwood had sung in the Spencer Davis Group and had been in Traffic for two years. And Rick Grech had played bass and violin in Family, a progressive British group from Leicester that never really succeeded in America. Picking up where Cream left off in 1968, the foursome recorded an immediately well received album that sold more than a million copies on the strength of standout tracks "Can't Find My Way Home" and "Presence of the Lord." Their debut gig in London's Hyde Park in June 1969 was highly anticipated and drew more than 100,000 fans.

But one group could not contain four such immense personalities, and egos clashed as they toured America. (Clapton even flew the coop one night to jam with John Lennon's Plastic Ono band in Toronto.) At tour's end, Blind Faith was history. Baker formed his short-lived Ginger Baker's Air Force, while Winwood reassembled Traffic. Clapton took up with the band's opening act, Delaney and Bonnie, and in 1970 released his first solo album.

Blind Faith: rock's first supergroup. Left: Eric Clapton and Steve Winwood. Top: from l
Ginger Baker, Rick Grech, Winwood, and Clapton. Above: Baker, Clapton, and Winwood.

JOE COCKER

Joe Cocker's unmistakable growl of a voice and keen choice of cover material made him a top draw in the seventies. He wasn't pretty to look at, but he sounded like no one else.

Cocker was born and reared in Sheffield, England, a steel town. By day, he worked for the East Midlands Gas Board. At night, he'd slip into a dark suit and bow tie and venture into the pubs to play drums for the Cavaliers, a skiffle group. By 1961, they had become the Avengers, with young Joe, calling himself Vance Arnold, stepping up to the microphone as their singer. They nearly stole the thunder from the Rolling Stones at a Sheffield City Hall gig in 1963 with a blend of originals and Ray Charles covers.

Joe's first single proper, a version of the Beatles' "I'll Cry Instead" by Joe Cocker's Big Blues, went absolutely nowhere. It wasn't until keyboardist Chris Stainton crossed tracks with Cocker to form the Grease Band that his career began to blossom. After some live exposure in London, Cocker earned a reputation as a fierce blues howler, and with special guests Jimmy Page and Steve Winwood, he recorded and released *With a Little Help From My Friends* in 1969. The album sailed to number sixty-eight on the American charts, where Cocker's tour included a television appearance on *The Ed Sullivan Show* and a memorable performance at the Woodstock Festival.

There's little doubt that it is Joe Cocker's sound, rather than his look, that draws audiences.

Cocker teamed with Leon Russell for a string of albums and tours, including one of the most bodacious concert treks ever undertaken, the *Mad Dogs and Englishmen* extravaganza (1970). Joined by no fewer than forty-three musicians, not counting a menagerie of girlfriends, children, crew members, a film crew, and, yes, a spotted dog, the exhausting tour drained Cocker of all energy. The mess did yield a film, a double-album set, and two hit singles, "The Letter" and "Cry Me a River," but Cocker continued to live dangerously. He drank excessively during a 1972 tour. On stage he forgot lyrics and had a difficult time keeping food in his stomach. Front-row ticket holders took their chances.

Cocker's only other huge single of the decade was "You Are So Beautiful" (1975), a ballad tenderly spun by that rough-hewn voice. His comeback in 1982 sent him to number one on the singles chart for the first time with "Up Where We Belong," a duet with pop singer Jennifer Warnes. He continues to perform into the nineties.

CREAM

When it comes to hard, blues-based rock and roll, no other group tore down more boundaries or was more influential than rock's first power trio, Cream. These guys wrote the book and laid the foundation for what was to become heavy metal. Extended jamming wasn't their only strength. They wrote hits, too. And everything came in threes: three men; three studio albums; three hit singles in the States; and only three years together.

Guitarist Eric Clapton was already the talk of the town after only a year as king shredder of John Mayall's Bluesbreakers. He had joined Mayall's band after leaving the Yardbirds, but was already growing restless. It was at this time that Clapton lent his talents to Powerhouse, a studio group that also included Steve Winwood.

Clapton was a big fan of bassist Jack Bruce. Bruce, who played the low notes for Alexis Korner's Blues Incorporated and the Graham Bond Organization, as well as doing a short stint alongside Clapton in the Bluesbreakers, had a potent style that Clapton adored. When Bond drummer

Jack Bruce (left) and Eric Clapton formed Cream in 1966 with drummer Ginger Baker. The band was history two years later, leaving behind three hit singles and three studio albums.

Peter "Ginger" Baker asked Clapton if he wanted to start a band, the guitarist agreed, but only if Bruce played bass. Though Baker and Bruce had an argument at the very first Cream meeting, the trio decided to give it a go.

At first, they stuck with straight blues numbers, but eventually evolved into more of a heavy commercial rock commodity with their debut, *Fresh Cream* (1966), and the follow-up, *Disraeli Gears* (1967). Both albums sold well in the States, and *Gears* yielded Cream's first single, "Sunshine of Your Love." The catchy rocker went all the way to number five in America, and provided many aspiring guitarists with their first lesson, courtesy of Clapton's memorable introduction.

Wheels of Fire (1968) came next. Felix Pappalardi, who later played in Mountain, was Cream's producer at this point, but for *Wheels* he joined in on the performance as well. Pappalardi also mixed more instruments into Cream and broadened their sound. Both the cello and marimbas can be heard on *Wheels*, as can a sixteen-minute version of "Toad" and their second and third singles, "White Room" and "Crossroads."

But that old bugaboo "creative differences" intervened, ultimately causing their demise. By mid-1968, Bruce and Baker were finding it more and more difficult to get along. On July 10, Clapton announced that the band would do one last tour, then pack it in.

The farewell swing began in Oakland, California, on October 5 and ended the next month. On November 26, Cream played its last concert before a packed house at London's Royal Albert Hall. (Progressive rockers Yes opened the show!) As the trio waved good-bye for the last time, the Brits shouted "God save the Cream!"

Posthumous releases followed, most notably *Goodbye Cream* in 1969. Clapton and Baker moved on to Blind Faith. Bruce took up a solo career.

DEREK AND THE DOMINOES

Had George Harrison's first wife, Pattie Boyd Harrison, not flirted with Cream guitarist Eric Clapton at the parties they occasionally attended, rock fans might never have heard one of classic rock's most enduring anthems, "Layla." Even though Clapton and Harrison were best friends, Clapton fell head over heels for the Beatle's wife, and though she eventually left Harrison for the guitar star, the miserable heartbreak that Clapton suffered can be heard in the grooves of Derek and the Dominoes' only studio venture, *Layla and Other Assorted Love Songs*, released to meager initial fanfare in 1970. "Bell Bottom Blues," "Why Does Love Have to Be So Sad?" "Have You Ever Loved a Woman?" and "Layla" all tell the heartrending story of a man imprisoned by his own passion.

Clapton had toured as special guest guitarist for Delaney and Bonnie and had released his first solo album before getting a call one day from their organist, Bobby Whitlock. Whitlock had had quite enough of the Bramlett's marital spats and wanted out. Clapton invited Whitlock to come to England and stay at his house, where the two jammed and wrote the core of the material for what would become the *Layla* album. Soon ex–Delaney and Bonnie buddies guitarist Dave Mason, bassist Carl Radle, and drummer Jim Gordon moved in, and the writing and jamming sessions intensified. After serving as the backing band for George Harrison's *All Things Must Pass* album, Derek and

Eric Clapton wrote "Layla" after reading *The Story of Layla and Majnun* by the Persian poet Nizami.

the Dominoes logged a brief tour of English clubs. Mason was only on hand for a few of those gigs.

When they were ready to record, the Dominoes flew to Miami to work with producer Tom Dowd, who Clapton treasured from his Cream days. When Clapton heard that Duane Allman, the guitarist who had graced Wilson Pickett's "Hey Jude," was playing in town with the Allman Brothers Band, he insisted they check the band out. Clapton and Allman, both guitar virtuosos, struck up a friendship, and after the Allmans finished their tour, Duane agreed to record with the Dominoes.

The addition of Duane Allman's slide guitar play kicked the Dominoes into high gear, and with a load of booze and dope on hand, the album was completed. Initially, Atlantic Records couldn't even get it on the radio, but in due time, it caught on.

Derek and the Dominoes began an extensive tour of America, with Duane present for only a few of the gigs, and recorded *In Concert*, a double live album, at New York's Fillmore East in October 1971. (It was not to be released until March 1973.) By the end of the tour, the Dominoes were using far too many drugs, and when they attempted to record a second project at London's Olympic Studios, the band broke down halfway through the proceedings and called it a day. Clapton grew more dependent on heroin, and secluded himself in his house for two and a half years. Clapton eventually married the only woman he's said he ever really loved, Pattie Boyd Harrison, but not until 1979, several years after the Dominoes' breakup. They divorced ten years later.

FLEETWOOD MAC

Of all the classic rock bands, no other outfit underwent more personnel and personality changes than Fleetwood Mac. Theirs is a unique fairy tale: while lead singers and guitarists came and went, the rhythm section stayed the course. And on the road to releasing one of classic rock's biggest-selling albums, *Rumours*, the trail was full of litigation, religious conversions, and in-house romances.

Peter Green was the guitarist who got the ball rolling in 1967. With drummer Mick Fleetwood, bassist Bob Brunning, and second guitarist Jeremy Spencer, they were just another British blues band. Brunning was soon replaced by John McVie, who had been part of John Mayall's Bluesbreakers with Green and Fleetwood. What to call themselves? Green had it all figured out. They'd use his full name, and add Mick's last name and a variation of the first syllable in McVie's last name. Peter Green's Fleetwood Mac played their debut gig at the British Jazz and Blues Festival in August 1967. It won them a recording contract.

The moniker didn't last long. Their 1968 debut album was credited only to Fleetwood Mac. Ignored in America, it won a following in the U.K. based on the hit single "Albatross," more a sullen instrumental than a traditional blues number. Guitarist Danny Kirwin came aboard for the band's second American album, *The Original Fleetwood Mac*, which was followed by three releases in 1969. *English Rose*, which includes the original "Black Magic Woman" (later borrowed by Carlos Santana), is the most memorable of the bunch, while *Then Play On* marked Green's last album with the band. Citing religious reasons, he left the music business alto-

Above left: Stevie Nicks (left) and Christine McVie, along with Lindsey Buckingham (above right), were part of Fleetwood Mac's most successful lineup. The band had survived several personnel changes before hitting on this winning combination.

gether, just as his composition "Green Manalishi" was gaining momentum for the band. Spencer was the next to find religion, and subsequently joined a group called the Children of God.

Enter singer/keyboardist Christine Perfect from the blues-rock band Chicken Shack. Actually, Perfect had performed uncredited on *Then Play On*, but couldn't legally join the band until 1971. By then she had married McVie. Her vocals on *Future Games*, especially on "Show Me A Smile," pointed the band in a fresh direction. Fleetwood Mac entered a muddled period at this point.

California guitarist Bob Welch was the next to join, followed by the ouster of Kirwin to make room for guitarists Dave Walker and Bob Weston. After the *Penguin* and *Mystery to Me* albums (both 1973), they, too, were history.

Here's where things get real sticky. A manager named Clifford Davies put together his own Fleetwood Mac with Walker and Weston and booked a U.S. tour. The real Fleetwood Mac filed an injunction against the band, eventually forcing them to change their name—they became Stretch. Protracted legal entanglements kept the original Fleetwood Mac off the road for most of 1974.

Fleetwood Mac relocated to California that same year, and in 1975, Welch tendered his resignation so that he could form his own group, Paris. Now Fleetwood and the McVies were on their own, until producer Keith Olsen played them the tapes for an album he had recently engineered for folk-rock duo

beauty of Nicks' "Rhiannon" and Christine McVie's "Say You Love Me." The McVies divorced in 1976, and Buckingham and Nicks separated not long after. But these romantic tensions led to the band's true watershed, *Rumours*, in 1977. The album might have veered dangerously close to easy-listening fluff, but it soared to number one in America, where it sat for a whopping thirty-one weeks, sold more than ten million copies, and gave the Sex Pistols and a new breed of punk rockers something to rebel against. (That same year, Peter Green was committed to a mental hospital for allegedly firing a gun at a messenger who was attempting to hand him a royalty check.)

Buckingham-Nicks. Fleetwood and the McVies were smitten, and hired singer/guitarist Lindsey Buckingham and his girlfriend, vocalist Stevie Nicks, along with Olsen, who would produce the next record. The Fleetwood Mac lineup with the million-dollar sound was finally intact. Not only did they have three strong songwriters, they had a genuine sex symbol in the sultry Nicks.

The born-again lineup released *Fleetwood Mac* in 1976, actually the second album from the band to bear that title. The album sold multimillions on the

Above left: Christine McVie (left) brought a more melodic sound when she joined the band in 1971; Lindsey Buckingham's strong guitar and studio expertise came along four years later. Above right: Charter member Mick Fleetwood has remained with the band through scores of tumultuous changes in principals, musical styles, and record labels.

It wasn't until two years later that Fleetwood Mac issued their next album, the highly ambitious and artistic double album, *Tusk*. With a million-dollar budget and a guest appearance by the University of Southern California's Trojan Marching Band, *Tusk*, recorded at L.A.'s Dodger Stadium, pointed Fleetwood Mac in yet another direction. The band closed the decade with another double set, this time a live album. *Live* was followed by *Mirage* in 1982, *Tango in the Night* in 1988, and *Behind the Mask* in 1989. By then, Mac's glory years were behind them.

VAN MORRISON

Through his early work with the blues-powered Them, Irishman Van Morrison wouldn't be out of place in the first half of this chapter, the early movement. But Them had little luck in the U.S., and it wasn't until Morrison went solo in 1967 that his career really took off.

An intensely private individual who seldom grants interviews, Van Morrison has been called many things: mystical poet, self-absorbed genius, religious seer, difficult head case, sensitive soul searcher. As at home with rhythm and blues as he is with a jazz instrumental or gospel hymn, this spiritual eclectic only marginally fits the definition of a rocker. As he once stated to the press about the likes of David Bowie and Mick Jagger, "I just can't figure them out."

Born George Ivan Morrison in 1945 in Belfast, Ireland, the son of Jehovah's Witnesses, he'd listen to his dad's jazz and blues records for hours on end. He learned guitar, saxophone, and harmonica on his own, and by the time he was sixteen, young Van was already touring Europe as the sax player for a rhythm-and-blues band called the Monarchs.

Back home in Ireland, the Monarchs retooled and became Them, the house band at Belfast's Maritime Hotel. Their first two singles, "Don't Start Crying Now" and a cover of Big Joe Williams' "Baby Please Don't Go," were hits in the U.K., but it wasn't until the release of "Here Comes the Night" in 1965 that the band began to draw notice in America. A follow-up, "Mystic Eyes," was not as strong.

Them's lineup changed nearly as often as their clothes thanks to Morrison's brooding temper and an ignorant management team, who often supplanted the musicians with hired guns, one of them the busy, in-demand Jimmy Page. The entire Them legacy is full of hard luck and heartbreak. The song they're perhaps best known for, "Gloria," wasn't even a major hit in the States. It took a Chicago-area garage band, the Shadows of Knight, to ride "Gloria" up the charts to number ten in 1966.

Disillusioned by the record industry, Morrison left Them in 1967. He was wooed to a recording studio in New York later that year by "Here Comes the Night" songwriter Bert Berns, who had started his own label, called Bang. Morrison recorded his first solo hit with Berns, the wistful "Brown Eyed Girl," along with a few reels full of demos that would eventually become Morrison's first solo album, *Blowin' Your Mind*.

On those demos were also early versions of songs Morrison would include on his first record for Warner Bros., the intensely personal, romantically mystic *Astral Weeks*. Recorded in a whirlwind forty-eight-hour period, it was given raves by critics. Though not one of its eight tracks yielded a single, the album sold well in the States.

Jazz, rhythm and blues, the frequent appearance of a horn section, and more transcendental meditation were all hallmarks of Morrison's early-seventies catalog, used to best effect on *Moondance* and *His Band and the Street Choir* (both 1970), *Tupelo Honey* (1971), *St. Dominic's Preview* (1972), the live set *It's Too Late to Stop Now* (1974), *Wavelength* (1978), and *Into the Music* (1979). With *A Common One* in 1980, critics began to dismiss his work as pretentious, but Morrison continued to record throughout the decade. (Success in the singles department abandoned him after "Wild Night" in 1971.)

In concert, one could never be sure whether Morrison was enjoying himself. He'd follow a swing tune, say, "Jackie Wilson Said," with a meandering musical excursion to nowhere, and either be silent between songs or mumble his way through segues. At a 1979 show at New York's Palladium, he fled the stage halfway through the set. Just as in his music and lyrics, Morrison could never be bothered to explain his erratic actions. A truly mysterious character, his odd behavior never overshadowed his musical contributions. Morrison contiues to tour and record into the ninties, and will keep it up as long as he's inspired.

TRAFFIC

Traffic could never be pinned down to one form of rock. Their music rode down a number of different avenues: rhythm and blues, folk, jazz, even classical. The soulful voice front and center never changed, though. Steve Winwood's singing was instantly recognizable. When that reedy voice kicked in, you knew it was Traffic.

Winwood was something of a child prodigy when he sang with the Spencer Davis Group. All of sixteen when he joined, his vocals drove their two biggest singles, "Gimme Some Lovin'" and "I'm a Man," into the top ten. But Winwood wanted to do more with his talents, and the late-night jam sessions he participated in at the Elbow Room, a Birmingham club, gave him the confidence to branch out with his own group. One of these sessions, with Winwood, flute and saxophone player Chris Wood, guitarist Dave Mason (a Davis Group roadie), and drummer Jim Capaldi, went particularly well, and Traffic was born.

The four had actually recorded together before. All had played percussion on the Spencer Davis Group's "I'm a Man," but Traffic would be entirely their group, and much more adventurous than Davis'. They traveled to a farmhouse in Berkshire where they sequestered themselves for a six-month rehearsal period, but it wasn't as pastoral as it sounds. Years later, Winwood confided that they were just four teenagers living together in squalor.

Traffic's first album, *Mister Fantasy*, released in 1968 in the States, was a mixed bag of musical styles. Mason was gone after the album's release, only to join again for another intense production period and their second release, *Traffic*, which included his classic composition "Feelin' Alright." At this point, the band broke up. Winwood formed Blind Faith with Eric Clapton. The others joined organist Mick Weaver as Mason, Capaldi, Wood, and Frog (Weaver was Frog). Leftover Traffic cuts were issued as *Last Exit*, and a greatest-hits album, *Best of Traffic*, should have been their swan song.

But after Blind Faith went belly-up, Winwood returned to England to begin work on a solo album to be called *Mad Shadows*. After laying down two songs, he first called in Capaldi to help with lyrics, then Wood—and Traffic was back. *John Barleycorn Must Die*, their fifth album and perhaps their best, was jazzier than previous releases and paved the way for the live album *Welcome to the Canteen* and *The Low Spark of High Heeled Boys*, both in 1971.

Personnel changes continued, and the group recorded a few more titles before disbanding in 1974 with *As the Eagle Flies*. Capaldi's solo career never really panned out, but Winwood struck gold on his own with a self-titled solo debut in 1977, *Arc of a Diver* (1980), *Talking Back to the Night* (1982), *Back in the High Life* (1986), and more. Wood died in 1983 after a long illness.

THE CALIFORNIA SONS

The British bands picked up the beat and gave American kids something to shake and shimmy about as Beatles fan clubs sprouted up across the country. Subsidiary businesses began to bloom, all thanks to rock and roll. Sheet music, fan magazines, lunch boxes, board games, and countless souvenirs were scarfed up by kids of all ages. Even fashion changed: Beatles boots and Beatles haircuts began to appear.

If the Brits could do it, so could Americans. The Beach Boys, in their early incarnation, epitomized the teenage American dream. What was more fun than headin' to the beach, catchin' a wave, cruisin' for girls? A considerable number of American kids living in the heartland could see a breaking wave only in movies like *Beach Blanket Bingo*, but they could slip on a Beach Boys record at any time and become part of the surf scene.

In the mid-sixties, popular American rock was still pretty tame. The Four Seasons, the Righteous Brothers, and Gary Lewis and the Playboys were riding high on the singles charts, as were the Supremes and the Four Tops. But later in the decade, American music grew more adventurous, and California became a hotbed for innovative rock and roll: Buffalo Springfield pioneered folk rock on the Pacific coast; the Eagles expanded it; later, the Doobie Brothers' country boogie won immense popularity. And through it all, Creedence Clearwater Revival, out of El Cerrito, became one of rock's biggest singles bands. The promise of the West, so central to the American cultural myth, had extended its provenance to rock and roll, and music would never be the same.

CCR's John Fogerty; Joe Walsh of the Eagles; the Beach Boys' Mike Love.

THE BEACH BOYS

Call them the ambassadors of the California surf sound, the golden boys who rhapsodized over cars, girls, and catchin' a wave, or even the most popular and influential American group in rock history and you're getting only half the picture. Beneath the velvet harmonies, cherubic smiles, sun-bleached hair, and good vibrations lies classic rock's most melodramatic soap opera, fraught with illicit subplots of drug addiction, mental illness, child abuse, alcoholism, and allegations of brainwashing.

Brian Wilson was the eldest of the three Wilson boys. As the brothers have repeated in interviews throughout their career, Brian was the Beach Boys; the others were simply his messengers. Only the middle brother, Dennis, was a real surfer boy. Carl was the pudgy baby, Brian's sidekick in the studio and eventual leader of the touring band. When Dennis suggested to his elder brother that he write a song about the new fad sweeping the West Coast, Brian wrote down every surfin' phrase he knew and set it to music. The result was "Surfin'."

Growing up in Hawthorne, California, the Wilson boys had already played local gigs as Carl and the Passions and Kenny and the Cadets. Brian taught his brothers and their cousin Mike Love to sing, first aping the four-part harmonies he'd nick from records by the Four Freshmen. The fifth original

The Beach Boys (from left: Dennis Wilson, Brian Wilson, Mike Love, Al Jardine, and Carl Wilson) embodied the California sound of the sixties with songs about surfin', cars, and girls.

member, guitarist Al Jardine, was a friend of Brian's from Hawthorne High, and the five agreed to call themselves the Pendletones before hitting on the surfing theme.

Adding barbershop harmonies to a surf guitar sound originated by local California guitar hero Dick Dale, "Surfin'" was released on the independent X label, later to be called Candix, in 1961. Changing their name to the Beach Boys, they earned three hundred dollars from their first gig, part of a Ritchie Valens memorial concert on New Year's Eve, 1961. "Surfin'" gained momentum and turned into a minor hit, but royalty payments were paltry. When the Candix label folded, Jardine enrolled in dental school, certain the Beach Boys were a passing fad. David Marks, a neighborhood friend, replaced him, but for only a year. By mid-1963, Jardine was back.

Brian Wilson was certain he was onto something big. So was his father, Murry—the boys' first manager and a failed songwriter himself—even though he hated "Surfin'." Murry was a bellowing tyrant, a strict disciplinarian who pushed the boys to their limits. Years into their success, Brian admitted in interviews that his hearing handicap—he has only 6 percent hearing capability in his right ear—might have been the result of a severe blow to the side of the head administered by Murry when the boy was only two years old.

Tyrant or not, Murry did engineer a recording contract for the Beach Boys with the Capitol label. From 1962 to 1966, they hit the top forty twenty-one times with songs about girls, cars, and surfin', most notably "Surfin' U.S.A." (so close to Chuck Berry's "Sweet Little Sixteen" that he shared a writing credit), "Surfer Girl," "Be True to Your School" (complete with a cheerleading squad), "Fun, Fun, Fun," "I Get Around" (their first number one hit), "Help Me, Rhonda," "California Girls," and "Barbara Ann."

In the studio, Capitol executive Nik Venet produced their first songs with Brian at his side. All production chores were turned over to Brian beginning with the third album, *Surfer Girl*. In concert, Brian played bass, Dennis played the drums, Carl played lead guitar, Al strummed rhythm guitar, and lead singer Mike Love served as unofficial emcee. Between the producing, songwriting (some of the titles were cowritten with Love and/or Gary Usher), arranging, and teaching the boys their parts, the touring became too much for Brian. In December 1964, at age twenty-two, he nearly suffered a nervous breakdown and was replaced on the road by Glen Campbell. Campbell wanted to be a star on his own, however, and was Beach Boys history three months later. Bruce Johnston, who had played with Phil Spector on "To Know Him Is to Love Him," was the next Beach Boy and became a permanent member.

After hearing the Beatles' *Rubber Soul*, Brian went to work on what has become the Beach Boys' masterpiece, *Pet Sounds*. Recorded in 1966 with a full orchestra, the album shunned the cars-and-surf theme for more mature, introspective songs. It reached number ten on the album charts and, years later, is the Beach Boys album many fans hold closest to their hearts.

Other fans insist that the 1966 single "Good Vibrations" was the pinnacle of the Beach Boys' success. Called "a pocket symphony" by Brian, the song displayed every last studio recording trick that he learned, took six months and sixteen thousand dollars to record, and became the first Beach Boys single to move a million copies.

Brian's peculiar and paranoiac behavior, exacerbated by excessive drug use, only increased during this period. He had a sandbox built around the grand piano in his den so that he could feel the fine grains beneath his feet as he composed. He insisted that business meetings be held in his backyard swimming pool to escape any bugs he suspected his father of planting in the house. He claimed to be receiving secret messages from Phil Spector. During a recording of "Fire," part of "The Elements" from the aborted *Smile* album, he forced the orchestra members to wear fire helmets just like his. When a batch of unusual fires broke out in L.A., he assumed the blame and canceled the project.

A lapse in popularity didn't help Brian's mental state. The late sixties and early seventies were lean years for the Beach Boys. The public had moved on to more progressive fare and viewed the boys from Hawthorne, California, as a nostalgia act. When the group canceled its Saturday night closing spot at the Monterey Pop Festival in 1967, many felt that the band was just plain scared of the competition. The next night, Jimi Hendrix told the audience, "You've heard the last of surf music."

Personnel changes in the band didn't help, until the release of *15 Big Ones* in 1976, which marked Brian's return to the production board. Since 1967's *Smiley Smile* LP, liner notes had read "Produced by the Beach Boys." Now Brian was back at the helm. He even rejoined them on the road in 1977, but now other conflicts came into play. Brian's psychotherapist, Dr. Eugene Landy, was accused of brainwashing him. Brian couldn't make a single decision without Landy's consent, and Landy's demand for half of Wilson's publishing royalties set in motion a series of lawsuits that continued well into the eighties.

Other problems persisted as well, particularly between Dennis Wilson and Mike Love. Earlier in their career, Love had discovered that his wife, Suzanne, had been having an affair with Dennis. Now Love was meditating with Maharishi Mahesh Yogi and, to everyone's chagrin, was encouraging all to join him. Dennis, plagued by marital problems, grew more dependent on alcohol and heroin, and by 1983 was having an affair with Love's daughter, Shawn. He drowned on December 28, 1983, after diving off a friend's boat in Marina Del Rey. The Beach Boys, continuing without him, did what other classic rock bands have done: hit gold with a soft-rock song. In their case, it was "Kokomo" and served as their last number one hit, in 1988.

BUFFALO SPRINGFIELD

Two albums and two years was all it took for Buffalo Springfield to lay down the blueprint for folk-country rock and spawn a new generation of rockers with more traditional roots.

Buffalo Springfield began as the Herd. Stephen Stills and Richie Furay had already worked together with the Au Go Go Singers in New York and had landed in Los Angeles to find a steady gig. (Stills had had an unsuccessful audition with the Monkees.) Legend has it that while stuck in an L.A. traffic jam, the two suspected that the gentleman driving the Pontiac hearse with the Ontario license plates in front of them was Neil Young, whom they knew from the Canadian coffeehouse circuit. It was Neil all right, with bassist and fellow Canadian Bruce Palmer in tow. Next thing, Young and Palmer were up in Stills and Furay's apartment working out a version of Young's "Nowadays Clancy Can't Even Sing" and it was decided on the spot to form a band. Adding ex-Dillard Dewey Martin on drums, the Herd eventually became Buffalo Springfield and the regular house band at Whisky-A-Go-Go on the Sunset Strip.

After months of tours with the Byrds and sometimes the Beach Boys, Buffalo Springfield's stunning debut album was released in early 1967 and yielded the band's only hit single,

Buffalo Springfield's "For What It's Worth" was a call to arms for a burgeoning youth movement full of free spirits, and it won the band immense credibility.

"For What It's Worth," a rallying cry penned by Stills. Unfortunately, problems hounded them from the start, and they never followed through with another hit.

During the recording of an unreleased second album, *Stampede*, Palmer's visa expired. Forced to return to Canada, other bassists came and went before the band finally settled on Jim Messina. By the time the offical follow-up album, the arguably better *Buffalo Springfield Again*, was released in 1968, internal battles, especially between Stills and Young, were pulling the band apart.

In March 1968, Young announced his decision to go solo but didn't officially depart until making a few more appearances with the band. One was at an L.A. police precinct, where he, Furay, Messina, and Eric Clapton were brought in after being busted for "being at a place where it is suspected marijuana is being used." Toward the end, guitarist Jim Hastings sat in when Neil wouldn't show for a gig. David Crosby from the Byrds also joined Springfield once or twice, until May 5, 1968, when Buffalo Springfield played its final concert, in Long Beach, California. Stills took up with Crosby and the Hollies' Graham Nash. Neil embarked on a long, rewarding solo career and a number of diverse side projects, including a spin with Crosby, Stills and Nash. Furay and Messina formed Poco with pedal steel player Rusty Young. Fans hoping for a Buffalo Springfield reunion have missed several informal private sessions at Stills' house with all the original members present.

CREEDENCE CLEARWATER REVIVAL

They were one of classic rock's greatest singles bands —thirteen top-forty hits in slightly less than four years—but it was never unhip to like Creedence Clearwater Revival. No matter how many seven-inch (17.7cm) slabs of vinyl they released and despite being in constant rotation on top-forty AM radio, Creedence was always perceived as a serious rock band.

No other outfit mixed a swamp-boogie sound into straight rock so effortlessly; John Fogerty's raw vocals and guitar craft were unique for their time. True, CCR came from a San Francisco suburb and hit their stride during the peace-and-love explosion, but psychedelia was clearly not an ingredient in their rock-from-the-bayou gumbo. Political and cultural issues, however, were. What's more, they were the original flannel-shirt rock band, predating the grunge movement by nearly two decades.

CCR was by no means an overnight sensation; their earliest recordings date as far back as 1959. The Fogerty boys, John and his elder brother Tom, were born and raised in Berkeley, California,

Travelin' band: Creedence Clearwater Revival toured worldwide and in one four-year period logged thirteen top-forty singles.

but were schooled in the East Bay suburb of El Cerrito. Tom always played guitar; John studied piano in his youth, and by age twelve was playing guitar as well. At junior high, they teamed with Stu Cook on bass and Doug "Cosmo" Clifford on drums and called themselves the Blue Velvets. Not only did they play local dances, they recorded for a label called Orchestra.

In 1964, Saul Zaentz of Fantasy records offered the band a deal, pro-vided they change their name to the Golliwogs. They reluctantly agreed, and recorded a string of singles for Fantasy, one of which, "Brown Eyed Girl," became a local hit. Follow-ups failed, and it wasn't until 1967 and a name change to Creedence Clearwater Revival—to better suit their swamp-rock boogie— that the Fogerty boys attracted a national audience.

Their self-titled 1968 debut album was full of strong John Fogerty compositions, but it was with two cover versions that Creedence hit the singles charts for the first time. "Suzie Q. (Part One)," an oldie from Dale Hawkins' repertoire, went all the way to number eleven. The follow-up, Screamin' Jay Hawkins' "I Put a Spell on You," was not as successful.

CLASSIC ROCK

every one of them a top-ten smash. But singles weren't their only strength. Their first album of 1970, *Cosmo's Factory*, proved that CCR could improvise with the best of 'em with an eleven-minute version of "I Heard It Through the Grapevine," an earlier soul hit for both Marvin Gaye and Gladys Knight and the Pips.

Enter that old crippler, internal dissension. John Fogerty was playing an increasingly dominant role in the band, and in January 1971, brother Tom offered his resignation. CCR continued on as a trio and toured nationwide, but by October 1972, the jig was up.

Three strong albums were released in 1969, all reflecting Fogerty's knack of writing immensely popular hit singles. *Bayou Country* yielded his first hit, "Proud Mary." (Two years later, Ike and Tina Turner turned it into their biggest hit.) From *Green River* came the title track, as well as "Lodi" and "Bad Moon Rising." *Willy and the Poor Boys* included the double-sided hit "Down on the Corner" backed with "Fortunate Son." By the time they earned ten thousand dollars playing the Woodstock festival in August 1969, they were one of America's most successful rock bands. Everyone knew at least one Creedence song.

The good times rolled through 1970 and 1971 with more hit singles: "Travelin' Band" backed with "Who'll Stop the Rain," "Up Around the Bend," "Lookin' Out My Back Door," "Have You Ever Seen the Rain," and "Sweet Hitch-Hiker,"

CCR (from left: Tom Fogerty, Stu Cook, Doug Clifford, and John Fogerty) maintained their image as noncommercial even as they produced hit after hit.

Mardi Gras, the first Creedence album to allow Cook and Clifford as much creative control as John Fogerty, was poorly received. The band called it a day.

Tom Fogerty released several solo albums and sat in with Jerry Garcia, among others, as a session musician. Tom died of a heart attack in September 1991. Brother John recorded as the Blue Ridge Rangers in 1973, and released his first solo album in 1975 on the Asylum label.

Fantasy continued issuing CCR albums, some without proper care. A 1970 concert recorded in Oakland was mistakenly released as *Live at Albert Hall*, later amended to *The Concert*. Fogerty, never a fan of Saul Zaentz, set his objections to music with the biting "Zanz Kant Danz," the final track on his 1985 solo release, *Centerfield*. After litigation proceedings by Zaentz, the title was changed to "Vanz Kant Danz" on later pressings.

THE DOOBIE BROTHERS

Neither critics' darlings nor sonic innovators, the Doobie Brothers deserve mention largely because of their tremendous popularity in the mid-seventies: "Long Train Runnin'," "China Grove," and "Black Water" are all staples of classic rock. Michael McDonald's entrance into the band in 1975 proved to be perfect timing. The second wind he brought to the band, albeit a sugary white-boy funk-pop, catapulted the Doobies back to the top of the charts with songs like "Takin' It to the Streets" and "What a Fool Believes."

When a San Jose band called Pud threw in the towel in 1969, members Tom Johnston, a singer/guitarist, and John Hartman, a drummer, began a series of Sunday afternoon open jams with bassist Dave Shogren and guitarist/singer Pat Simmons. Taking the name the Doobie Brothers, the band became a Hell's Angels favorite and quickly secured a record deal with Warner Bros.

Their self-titled debut album in 1971 fell flat, but after a personnel tune-up that added Michael Hossack and Tiran Porter, their next releases,

There was no one named Doobie in the Doobie Brothers. The San Jose band took their name from the slang term for a marijuana cigarette.

Toulouse Street and *The Captain and Me*, kicked off a long career with the infectious hits "Listen to the Music" and "Jesus Is Just Alright." Critics argued that the band was just rewriting the same song over and over again, but the public couldn't get enough.

By 1975, Steely Dan guitarist Jeff "Skunk" Baxter was a full-time Doobie, and when a stomach ailment sidelined Johnston, another ex–Steely Dan member, singer/keyboardist Michael McDonald, came off the bench. With the release of the immensely popular *Minute by Minute* in 1978, it was clear that the Doobies were now McDonald's baby. His instantly recognizable tenor voice replaced the silken harmonies and sharp, rapid guitar strum (which opened more than one Doobie classic) as the band's trademark.

At the turn of the decade, the Doobies abruptly and surprisingly disappeared from radio airwaves. Reunions in 1988 and 1991 were halfhearted attempts at best.

THE EAGLES

In the sixties, California rock meant surfing the big wave, cruising in the Woody, and pickin' up your date at eight. By the seventies, a whole new side of the California sound had evolved. California rock still mirrored the West Coast lifestyle, but it was, like it or not, mellow. No one captured the movement as precisely as the Eagles did.

Had Glenn Frey not asked Don Henley in 1971 to join Linda Ronstadt's touring band, the Eagles might never have taken flight. But Henley's band at the time, Shiloh, was stuck in low gear, and he needed the two hundred bucks a week that Ronstadt was offering. After beers at the Troubadour bar, Henley agreed to audition. He passed with flying colors and struck up a friendship with Frey on the road. After playing together on Ronstadt's 1971 release, *Silk Purse*, the duo decided to carry on.

With Frey playing guitar and piano and Henley on drums (both sang), the two teamed with Bernie Leadon from the Flying Burrito Brothers and Randy Meisner from Poco. Meisner played bass; Leadon was equally proficient on guitar, banjo, and mandolin. The Eagles' 1972 self-titled debut album captured the country-rock sound they were after and went gold on the strength of a Frey collaboration with Jackson Browne, "Take It Easy."

Fans scarfed up the Eagles' new California sound, such a "peaceful, easy feeling."

Desperado (1973) was equally well received, and for *On the Border* (1974), the band added yet another guitarist, session veteran Don Felder. With *One of These Nights* (1975), the Eagles were moving toward rock and away from country, which signaled Leadon's exit.

One of rock's truly rambunctious characters, Joe Walsh from the James Gang, then provided a much-needed kick, and the Eagles reached their summit. *Hotel California*, Walsh's debut, was their third number one album in a row, selling more than eleven million copies worldwide and spawning huge hits with the title track and "Life in the Fast Lane."

By 1977, Timothy B. Schmidt had replaced Meisner, but it took two years and a million-dollar budget to complete *The Long Run*. The title track, as well as "Heartache Tonight" and "I Can't Tell You Why," reached the top ten on the singles charts, and the band drew turn-away crowds everywhere they played, but offers of solo projects were too tempting.

After a live album in 1980, the Eagles flew their separate ways. Henley's solo career has outdistanced those of his colleagues. As for Walsh, the titles of his solo ventures (such as *The Smoker You Drink, the Player You Get*) are more memorable than the material inside. His "Rocky Mountain Way" and "Life's Been Good," however, are fixtures of classic rock. A 1994 reunion tour drew sell-out crowds, a testament the Eagles' lasting popularity.

THE MAMAS AND THE PAPAS

They honed their craft playing New York City's Greenwich Village club circuit, but how could the group that sang "California Dreamin'" be left out of this chapter?

The Mamas and the Papas combined smooth harmonies with strong songwriting from John Phillips into a short-lived but impressive run. They came off like hippies, but their records were as much pop as folk rock.

A clump of hit singles followed: "Monday, Monday," "I Saw Her Again," "Words of Love," "Dedicated to the One I Love," and "Creeque Alley." These hippies sold albums, too—*If You Can Believe Your Eyes and Ears* (1966) and *The Mamas and the Papas* (1967) both sold a million. And in 1967 John and Michelle organized the hugely successful Monterey Pop Festival.

They played only thirty concerts together, but the public could

Singers Cass Elliot and Dennis Doherty had been in the Mugwumps. Phillips, a guitarist, and his wife, Michelle, wed in 1962, and were in the New Journeymen, a folk group that had gone through a number of name changes. By 1965, the four were in Los Angeles and down on their luck. While singing background vocals on a Barry McGuire album, *This Precious Time*, they scored a deal with Dunhill records and released "California Dreamin'," a Phillips composition sung by Doherty. (Barry McGuire recorded the song as well and used the same instrumental and backup vocal tracks.) The single made it all the way to number four.

From New York they came, to sing "California Dreamin'": (from left) Denny Doherty, "Mama" Cass Elliot, Michelle Phillips, and John Phillips.

often see them on television. *The Ed Sullivan Show*, *Shindig*, *The Hollywood Palace with Arthur Godfrey*, and *American Bandstand* all booked the Mamas and the Papas, and although they looked like such groovy peaceniks together, there was dissension within. After Michelle and Denny had an affair, Michelle left the group. She was back in soon enough, but it was all downhill after 1968. The Mamas and the Papas re-formed for an ill-received reunion in 1971, and Elliot, no doubt their best singer, continued on a solo career until her death in 1974.

STREETS OF SAN FRANCISCO

By July 1967, America was a nation in generational turmoil. The death toll of the Vietnam War had risen to more than twelve thousand. Free-thinking teenagers couldn't understand what America was doing fighting another country's battle. The Selective Service had already called up a good number of men for immediate physical and mental examinations. Now Uncle Sam could be coming after *you*. In retaliation, the motto "Make Love Not War" became a rallying cry as the Jefferson Airplane sang "Don't you want somebody to love?" The Airplane instructed, "One pill makes you larger and one pill makes you small. And the ones that mother gives you don't do anything at all. Go ask Alice when she's ten feet tall." Kids were turning on to a new breed of psychedelics—both rockers and pharmaceutical mind-expanders—as marijuana, LSD, mushrooms, and all sorts of colored tablets became more accessible.

And it all came together in San Francisco. Was it the cheap housing? Or was it all due to one Augustus "Owsley" Stanley III—an, ah, chemist, who manufactured a variety of hallucinogens in his San Fran laboratory, available at no charge? It was a combination of all these factors that turned the Bay Area into the chief nesting ground for the psychedelic era in late 1966 and made it *the* town for many a be-in and freak-out during the Summer of Love in 1967.

The addresses are nearly as renowned as the groups who communed within: 2400 Fulton Street (Jefferson Airplane's hangar), 710 Ashbury Street (the Grateful Dead's hangout), 746 Brannan (the initial headquarters of *Rolling Stone* magazine), the corner of Fillmore and Geary (home of the Fillmore West concert hall) and the quaint, celebrated Haight-Ashbury district, where you could let it all hang out. In late 1967, you could have walked into any one of these spots and felt the good vibes, or at least smelled them.

Free spirits like Tom "Big Daddy" Donohue launched progressive, free-form radio at KMPX-FM. Concert promotor Bill Graham jump-started many rock-star careers. Journalist Ralph J. Gleason championed many psychedelic groups in the *San Francisco Chronicle* and later launched *Rolling Stone* with Jann Wenner, after talking Wenner out of naming the magazine *The Electric Newspaper*. And then there were the big groups who spread to the rest of the nation San Francisco's gospel of peace, love, and whatever turns you on.

The Grateful Dead's Jerry Garcia; Grace Slick of the Jefferson Airplane; Janis Joplin.

COUNTRY JOE AND THE FISH

One of the first acts to emerge from beyond the Golden Gate with a rocked-up bagful of protest songs was Country Joe and the Fish, led by the flamboyant Joe McDonald. You couldn't fit another protest button on Joe's shirt. He even took the lyrics to Scott McKenzie's song "San Francisco" to heart and wore flowers in his hair. And Joe's group of psychedelic merrymakers, more of a jug band at the start than a rock outfit, shunned the traditional two-party government system for one big party! You couldn't throw a rock festival without inviting Country Joe and the Fish.

Joe, named by his liberal parents after Joseph Stalin, was a fixture of the Berkeley sixties scene. By 1966, his motley crew of musicians, the Fish, were intact with a wardrobe of funny costumes and a well-oiled stage act complete with get-out-of-Vietnam sing-alongs and mock commercials for various illegal substances. By 1967, they were at every rock and pop festival in the States, stealing the show with their infamous F-U-C-K cheer, the prelude to their "Feel-Like-I'm-Fixin'-To-Die Rag," something of a national anthem for the antiwar movement. The chant landed them in trouble more than once. At the Democratic convention in 1968, Joe and his two guitarists, Barry Melton and David Cohen, were confronted in an elevator by a trio of Vietnam veterans who challenged, "Don't

The very first song the highly political Joe McDonald wrote was a campaign song—called "I Seen a Rocket"—for his high school buddy's run at the class presidency.

you like America?" In 1969, the Fish were arrested in Worcester, Massachusetts, for inciting lewd behavior. Following that incident, promoters grew wary, and the band's bookings decreased.

Following breakups and reunions with the Fish, Country Joe took up the liberal cause with Jane Fonda and Donald Sutherland in a traveling road show dubbed FTA (Fuck the Army). The Fish often regrouped during the seventies, but by then they came off more like a novelty act than a political statement.

THE
GRATEFUL
DEAD

The Grateful Dead have outgrown the mantle "Kings of Psychedelic Rock." They are the grand-daddies of the entire classic rock genre. No other band has remained as consistently active as the Dead. No other classic rockers are held in such reverence by their fans. No other act sells as many concert tickets year in, year out. While

The Grateful Dead (from left: Phil Lesh, Bill Kreutzmann, Bob Weir, Mickey Hart, and Jerry Garcia) testified to their longevity with lyrics like "Oh well, a touch of grey kinda suits you anyway" and "We will survive" on their 1987 LP, *In the Dark*.

musical tastes twist and change and stylistic fads come and go, the Dead have survived it all and show no sign of losing their grip.

Through twenty-three album releases and a countless number of bootleg recordings, through various personnel changes, drug busts, rehab efforts, and through tour after tour of marathon

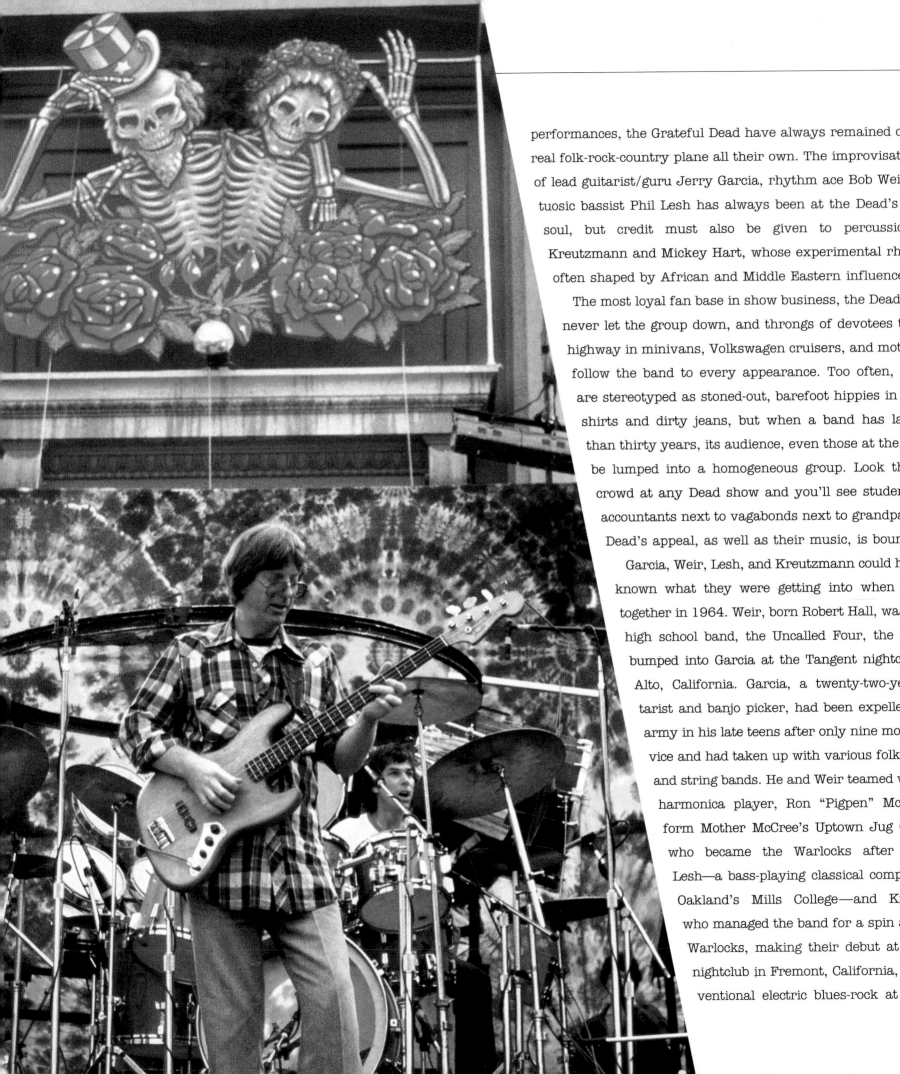

performances, the Grateful Dead have always remained on an ethereal folk-rock-country plane all their own. The improvisational style of lead guitarist/guru Jerry Garcia, rhythm ace Bob Weir, and virtuosic bassist Phil Lesh has always been at the Dead's heart and soul, but credit must also be given to percussionists Bill Kreutzmann and Mickey Hart, whose experimental rhythms are often shaped by African and Middle Eastern influences.

The most loyal fan base in show business, the Deadheads, has never let the group down, and throngs of devotees take to the highway in minivans, Volkswagen cruisers, and motor bikes to follow the band to every appearance. Too often, Deadheads are stereotyped as stoned-out, barefoot hippies in tie-dyed T-shirts and dirty jeans, but when a band has lasted more than thirty years, its audience, even those at the core, can't be lumped into a homogeneous group. Look through the crowd at any Dead show and you'll see students next to accountants next to vagabonds next to grandparents. The Dead's appeal, as well as their music, is boundless.

Garcia, Weir, Lesh, and Kreutzmann could hardly have known what they were getting into when they came together in 1964. Weir, born Robert Hall, was still in his high school band, the Uncalled Four, the evening he bumped into Garcia at the Tangent nightclub in Palo Alto, California. Garcia, a twenty-two-year-old guitarist and banjo picker, had been expelled from the army in his late teens after only nine months of service and had taken up with various folk, bluegrass, and string bands. He and Weir teamed with a blues harmonica player, Ron "Pigpen" McKernan, to form Mother McCree's Uptown Jug Champions, who became the Warlocks after dealing in Lesh—a bass-playing classical composer out of Oakland's Mills College—and Kreutzmann, who managed the band for a spin as well. The Warlocks, making their debut at a cramped nightclub in Fremont, California, played conventional electric blues-rock at the outset, but a year later were experimenting in improvisational and tangential excursions, both musical and otherwise.

Suspecting there was another band already called the Warlocks, they decided a name change was in order. According to one story, at a mind-expanding smoking session at Lesh's house, Garcia stuck his thumb into the pages of the *Oxford English Dictionary*, randomly opened to the page where the phrase "Grateful Dead" appeared—supposedly derived from an Egyptian prayer—and the Grateful Dead they became.

By 1967, the Dead were living at 710 Ashbury Street and playing free shows in Golden Gate Park as well as steady gigs at the Avalon Ballroom and Bill Graham's Fillmore West. As the house band at Ken Kesey's Acid Tests—a series of open LSD parties—they took on psychedelic overtones. That same year, they were signed to the Warner Bros. label and released their debut album before relocating to Marin County and adding Mickey Hart.

The Dead's early albums—*Grateful Dead*, *Anthem of the Sun*, *Aoxomoxoa*—found a home with followers, but on vinyl the band couldn't convey the communal mood or the alchemic energy pumped out at their performances, which included landmark appearances at the Monterey Pop Festival in 1967, the Miami Pop Festival in 1968, and Woodstock in 1969. Even their many live albums through the seventies failed to capture the concert magic. It wasn't until *Workingman's Dead* and *American Beauty*, both released in 1970, that the records stood up to the shows. Songs from this era—"Casey Jones," "Sugar Magnolia," "Truckin'"—remain concert favorites to this day.

A long strange trip: bassist Phil Lesh (opposite) and rhythm guitarist Bob Weir (above) are charter members of the Dead, who began in 1964 as the Warlocks.

Pianist Keith Godchaux and his wife, singer Donna Jean, joined in 1971 and 1972, respectively, after the Dead lost Pigpen to liver cancer. During the next seven years, solo ventures and spinoff projects were as numerous as Dead records. Garcia recorded with jazz artists Howard Wales and Merle Saunders as well as on his own. Weir hooked up with Kingfish. Hart had his Diga Rhythm Band. In 1978, another phase began, with the release of *Shakedown Street*. The Dead, now on Arista Records, concentrated on shorter songs that seemed tailored for radio and, in the title track's case, the disco floor. Still, few Deadheads cried sellout. *Shakedown Street* was the Dead's last record of the seventies, but was by no means a permanent change in direction. In 1978, they played three concerts at the Great Pyramid in Egypt, recorded but never released, and closed out the decade where they are most at home—on the stage of a concert arena. Pianist Brent Mydland replaced the Godchauxs in 1979. (Godchaux died the next year in a car crash, and another tragedy occurred when Mydland was found dead in his home in 1990.)

From the parking-'n'-party lot to the "fan-recording zone" reserved for those devotees with a good tape deck and a huge collection of tradable cassettes, a Dead show is a communal homecoming for millions of worshipers who have grown up with the Dead's music, grown old with it, or plan to. This is truly a band for the ages. As long as Garcia and Weir are up for it, the Dead will never die.

THE JEFFERSON AIRPLANE

The Grateful Dead might have been the embodiment of the San Francisco sound, but the first Bay Area band to land a major record deal and spread the gospel of the Haight-Ashbury district to middle America was the Jefferson Airplane. When ex-model Grace Slick joined the band in the summer of 1966 (and brought two future hits, the band's biggest, with her), it was their ticket out of town. Singer Marty Balin was running the Matrix, a

Signe Toly Anderson (left, with the Jefferson Airplane) shared lead vocals with Marty Balin up until the release of their debut, *Jefferson Airplane Takes Off*, in September 1966. Pregnancy forced her to retire, and Grace Slick (right, with the band) was quickly enlisted.

nightclub on Fillmore Street, in 1965 when he met guitarist Paul Kantner and asked if he would be interested in starting a band. With sweet-voiced singer Signe Toly Anderson and exceptional guitar-picker Jorma Kaukonen, the team recruited a rhythm section in bassist Bob Harvey and drummer Skip Spence for a folk-rock sound not unlike the We Five's, who had a big hit that summer with "You Were on My Mind." Debuting in August of that year at the Matrix and soon becoming the house band, Balin and Kantner's troupe played the premier folk songs of the day by Bob Dylan, Gordon Lightfoot, and Fred Neil. Harvey was out early in the game, and Kaukonen brought in his buddy Jack Casady to play bass. Kaukonen also suggested a handle for the group, a shortened version of "Blind Thomas Jefferson Airplane," a name he dreamed up for both a fictional blues singer and a dog.

After *San Francisco Chronicle* writer Ralph J. Gleason identified the band in a glowing review as a vital ingredient to the burgeoning San Francisco scene, the Airplane received a twenty-five-thousand-dollar advance from RCA Victor Records, considered steep for the day, and issued their first record, *Jefferson Airplane Takes Off*, in September 1966. "It's No Secret" and "Blues from an Airplane" showcased Balin's and Anderson's strong vocals and rich harmonies, but Anderson would soon be history.

The band's growing legions of fans included Grace Slick, her husband Jerry, and brother-in-law Darby, who decided to form a band the very night they caught the Airplane. The Great Society never racked up any hits, but did build a local following of their own, courtesy of Slick's remarkable voice and powerful stage presence. When Anderson became pregnant and unable to tour just before the release of *Takes Off*, Slick came in. Anderson's hard-core fans wept, but without Slick, the Airplane would never have taken off. *Surrealistic Pillow* (1967), her first album with the band, marked a watershed, and the two hits Slick brought over from the Great Society, "Somebody to Love" (originally titled "Someone to Love") and "White Rabbit," became top-ten hits and Airplane staples. Skip Spence left during this period to form Moby Grape, and was replaced by former jazz drummer Spencer Dryden.

After Bathing at Baxter's (1967), *Crown of Creation* (1968), and a live album, *Bless Its Pointed Little Head* (1969), all kept the Airplane airborne, but *Volunteers*, released later in 1969, was their inarguable tour de force. With brothers-in-arms

Stephen Stills, Jerry Garcia, Nicky Hopkins, and David Crosby, the Airplane released their most accomplished batch of tunes, including "We Can Be Together," "Good Shepherd," "Wooden Ships," and the title track, and turned in showstopping performances at the Woodstock and Altamont festivals.

Here's where the splintering began: Dryden left to form the New Riders of the Purple Sage; Kaukonen and Casady formed Hot Shit, who changed their name to Hot Tuna; and Slick became pregnant by Kantner and was sidelined for a while. The housebound couple, along with members of the Dead, recorded *Blows Against the Empire*, something of a science fiction soundtrack, which became the first release for the Jefferson Starship and the springboard for the next phase of their career. Before the Airplane recorded *Bark* in 1971, Balin was gone as well. *Long John Silver* (1972) was the last gasp for the Airplane.

Slick's solo excursion, *Manhole*, failed to make a splash, and Kaukonen and Casady were devoting all their time to Hot Tuna. Officially calling themselves the Jefferson Starship, Slick, Kantner, a returning Balin, keyboardist David Freiberg, drummer John Barbata, bassist Pete Sears, and teenage guitarist Craig Chaquico recorded *Dragon Fly*, memorable for "Ride the Tiger" and "Caroline." Balin stuck around for their next release, the immensely popular *Red Octopus*—which climbed to number one and went multiplatinum on the strength of "Miracles"—but now the band was softening up considerably and some songs could even be played on adult contemporary stations. Even Slick acknowledged that the group had become too bland. After two more records, *Spitfire* (1976) and *Earth* (1978), and an ongoing bout with alcoholism, she left, as did Balin.

Solo careers continued for the two. The addition of singer Mickey Thomas (from the Elvin Bishop Group) to the Jefferson Starship did nothing to save their descent into mediocrity. Although Slick rejoined in 1981 and the band changed its name yet again, this time to just Starship, the hits "We Built This City," "Sara," and "Nothing's Gonna Stop Us Now," chart-toppers all, were nothing more than soft-rock pap.

JANIS JOPLIN

The classic rock roster is by and large a male club. Only a woman in possession of divine and extraordinary talents, one able to mix with the boys but maintain her own sensuality, could emerge from the glut of testosterone. Grace Slick, Joan Baez, Tina Turner, and several other free spirits come to mind, but the woman who mattered as much for who she was as for the strength of her music was the late Janis Joplin. She was rock's classic belter, the diva of white-girl blues, her legend full of boozy and sexual escapades, and she was gone way before her time.

Born in Port Arthur, Texas, on January 19, 1943, Joplin was indeed considered "one of the boys" in her hometown. She spewed vulgar language with the toughest of the street louts and even joined an all-male gang in high school. Her interest in music didn't develop until she enrolled at the University of Texas in Austin and first heard the passion of seminal folk artists Leadbelly, Odetta, and, most importantly, Bessie Smith, whom Janis treasured. Young Joplin sang with the Waller Creek Boys in Austin clubs, but her rough demeanor was unwelcome and she was derided at college. After the student body cruelly voted her "Ugliest Man on Campus" in 1963, she hitchhiked to San Francisco with a friend, Chet Helms, eventually made her way to New York, sang in a few Greenwich Village gin mills, got caught up in alcohol and speed, and was back in Port Arthur by 1965.

Joplin was about to join the 13th Floor Elevators—a psychedelic rock and roll band out of Austin that was later immortalized by singer Roky Erickson—but when Helms called in June 1966 and asked her to join Big Brother and the Holding Company, a band he was managing at the time, she jumped at the opportunity and returned to San Francisco.

Joplin hit it off with Big Brother from the get-go, and word of a white girl singing her soulful ass off in the Bay Area clubs soon spread through the community. Joplin didn't write many songs, but after her hardy, whiskey-laced voice sunk into Erma (Aretha's sister) Franklin's "Piece of My Heart," Big Mama Thornton's "Ball and Chain," and even the Bee Gees' "To Love Somebody," Joplin had every right to call those songs her own. By 1967, Big Brother was in good company, playing at the first human "be-in" in Golden Gate Park on January 14 with the Grateful Dead and the Jefferson Airplane. After two amazing sets at the Monterey Pop Festival in June, the band was signed to Columbia Records, and their first album, *Cheap Thrills* (amended from *Sex, Dope, and Cheap Thrills* at

Janis Joplin's posthumously released album *Pearl*—titled after Joplin's own nickname—featured one song with incomplete vocals. The singer died before she could finish recording "Buried Alive in the Blues."

the company's request), released in autumn 1968, stayed at number one for eight weeks.

Joplin's talents outgrew Big Brother, and by 1969 she was recording with the Kozmic Blues Band (taking only guitarist Sam Andrews with her), and appearing on television shows hosted by Dick Cavett, Tom Jones, and Ed Sullivan. But her dependency on heroin jeopardized every appearance. As fiery as her performance at Woodstock was, it paled in comparison to her earlier concerts. By year's end, the Kozmic Blues Band was history after releasing only one album with Janis, *I Got Dem Ol' Kozmic Blues Again Mama!*

She formed a new group in spring 1970, the Full Tilt Boogie Band, took to the road once more, and even kicked heroin for a while, but by September, during the studio sessions for her final album, *Pearl*, her bad habits had returned. On October 4, 1970, after barhopping the night away, Joplin returned to her room at L.A.'s Landmark Hotel, where she died of a heroin overdose at only twenty-seven. *Pearl* was released posthumously and yielded her only number one hit, "Me and Bobby McGee," a song written by former lover Kris Kristofferson.

Joplin's influence is immeasurable, evident not only in female belters like Bette Midler and Heart's Ann Wilson, but even more in white-boy blues rockers infatuated with her mystique, like Chris Robinson of the Black Crowes and Axl Rose of Guns N' Roses. Rock might never know a lonelier soul than Joplin. Her classic quotation, "Onstage, I make love to twenty-five thousand people. Then I go home alone," tells it all.

THE STEVE MILLER BAND

Like Joplin and so many others who gravitated to San Francisco in 1966, Steve Miller honed his chops in various locales before trying his luck in the Bay Area. Miller was never into psychedelia; his preference was the blues. When the seventies were over, the Steve Miller Band had racked up a canon of top-ten hits including "The Joker," "Rock'n Me," "Fly Like an Eagle," and "Jet Airliner." These guys owned the radio airwaves, both top-forty and album-oriented formats.

Steve Miller was a child prodigy. He was playing guitar before the age of twelve in his native Milwaukee (even learning some chords firsthand from T-Bone Walker and Les Paul, friends of his dad), and had his first band in place, the Marksmen Combo, by his teens. The other guitarist in the combo was young Boz Scaggs, who followed Miller into his next band, the Ardells, later to become the Fabulous Knight Trains.

After studying for a year in Denmark, then playing around the Chicago area, Miller landed in San Francisco and assembled the Steve Miller Blues Band ("Blues" was later dropped from the name). His old

Milwaukee native Steve Miller assembled the Steve Miller Blues Band in San Francisco, where they gathered a steady following by playing free outdoor concerts. They landed a record deal after a stellar performance at the 1967 Monterey Pop Festival.

friend Scaggs was aboard for a debut at the Matrix nightclub, and like Joplin, the band was a sensation at the 1967 Monterey Pop Festival, where they inked a deal with Capitol Records.

The first few Steve Miller Band albums received a great deal of airplay on progressive radio; the second yielded his first hit in "Livin' in the U.S.A." But in 1972, Miller broke his neck in a car crash, and a bout with hepatitis put recording and touring on hold through 1973. During this time, greatest-hits packages were selling well, instilling a determination in Miller to return even stronger and healthier. He did. *The Joker*, unveiled in 1973, revealed a new Steve Miller, a bit more slick and a lot more pop, though he still clung to his blues past. The album's title track resurrected "Maurice" and "The Gangster of Love," characters who had appeared in earlier Miller compositions. The new Steve Miller was even more radio-friendly than the first one. His next two records, *Fly Like an Eagle* (1976) and *Book of Dreams* (1977, his last for the decade), were megasellers and guaranteed him a foothold in the legacy of classic rock.

SANTANA

Before his death in 1991, concert promoter Bill Graham told a story about a seventeen-year-old Carlos Santana trying to break into the Fillmore West by climbing a drainpipe up to the marquee and sneaking in through a second-story window. Cream and the Butterfield Blues Band were on the bill that night, both favorites of Carlos. Although he and a buddy were broke, they had to see the show, and after identifying themselves to Graham as fledgling musicians, he let them slide.

Santana doesn't remember the episode, and says that Graham is mistaking him for someone else, but one thing is for sure: only one band headlined the Fillmore West before releasing a record. That band was Santana, who didn't sign with Columbia records until blowing minds at Woodstock in 1969 ("Soul Sacrifice" was their showstopper). Of the big Golden Gate bands of the day, Santana was the last out of town.

Graham loved Latin music, and was one of the first to book the Santana Blues Band, which took Carlos' name only because the musician's union required that someone be the leader. Santana was

Vocalists came and went through the years, but impassioned guitarist Carlos Santana was always at the helm. Santana remains the only band to headline the Fillmore West before releasing a record.

always hanging around the Fillmore, and if a band didn't show or was forced to cancel, Santana's group filled the spot. And they always won the crowd over. Always.

Santana came to San Francisco from his native Mexico, where he played guitar in the strip joints that lined a street in Tijuana called Revolución. By the early sixties, he was cutting out of high school, washing dishes in San Francisco's Latin District at Tick-Tock's on Third Street, and jamming with bassist David Browne, keyboardist Gregg Rolie, drummer Rod Harper, and second guitarist Tom Frazer. By 1969, the lineup included Michael Shrieve on drums and percussionists Mike Carabello and José Chepito Areas. Carlos rarely, if ever, sang, leaving vocal duties to Rolie at the start, Leon Thomas in the mid-seventies, and, eventually, Alex Ligertwood. In 1971, guitarist Neal Schon joined, but left two years later to form Journey with Rolie.

Through twenty-odd album releases—most notably *Santana*, the 1969 debut; *Abraxas* (1970); a live double LP in 1974, *Lotus* (available only as an import until later in the decade); nearly ten solo albums for Carlos; and huge hits in "Evil Ways," "Black Magic Woman," and "Oye Como Va"—Santana was the sole classic group to succeed on a steady diet of Latin rock.

THE PROGRESSIVES

Riots and protests against the Vietnam War continued on college campuses as President Lyndon Johnson announced in March 1968 that he would not seek the Democratic nomination for president of the United States. The music of Country Joe and the Jefferson Airplane played in the background as young America grew ever more liberated. In April 1968, police stormed five Columbia University buildings and arrested hundreds of students who had staged a week-long sit-in. Draft cards were burned; so were brassieres. In May 1968, the U.S. Supreme Court upheld the law that designated draft-card torching as a punishable crime.

In August, eight thousand demonstrators stormed the Democratic convention in Chicago and chanted "The whole world's watching" as police billy-clubbed and paddy-wagoned one kid after another. The band Chicago Transit Authority opened the fourth side of their debut album with an actual recording of the chant. Still, the Vietnam War grew uglier, and by April 1969, the death toll had surpassed that of the Korean War.

Protest rock was peaking and a new genre was just beginning to blossom. Enter progressive rock, with a slew of musicians eager to cram more words and notes into the basic rock tune. Songs grew longer and more intricate. Horn sections, orchestras, and exotic instruments were brought in. New technologies made the Moog synthesizer available to rockers. Subtlety and spontaneity may have taken a back seat, but this was where rock was heading.

In the process, a lot of great songs were ruined by excessive production, as bands got caught up in trying to outdo one another. Many, though, produced some terrific music.

Frank Zappa; Queen's Freddie Mercury; Ian Anderson of Jethro Tull.

BLOOD, SWEAT AND TEARS

Veteran keyboardist and singer Al Kooper had spent two years with the Blues Project, a New York–based blues revival band, and had played on Bob Dylan's *Highway 61 Revisited* album (and was even a member of the Royal Teen, who hit with "Short Shorts" in 1958) when the bug hit to assemble a rock band with a prominent horn section. Kooper had arranged and penned material for the Blues Project, but split after a second live album, only their third record overall, was recorded in 1967. The original Blues Project disbanded soon thereafter.

Blood, Sweat and Tears: pioneers of the jazz-rock movement, a short-lived genre that never caught on.

Kooper approached producer James William Guercio in mid-1967 with an idea for a new jazz-rock band featuring Kooper and members of his old band. But Kooper didn't want just a rock band with horns. He envisioned a brand-new sound, an outfit where the trumpet, trombone, and saxophone were as important as the guitar. But Guercio, who had produced hits and worked successfully with horns with the Buckinghams, was already conspiring to produce his own jazz-rock outfit with an old friend, saxophonist Walter Parazaider.

The jazz-rock race was on. Although Guercio and Parazaider's band, the Big Thing, was formed in February 1967, and Blood, Sweat and Tears didn't come together until several months later,

BS&T won the race to the record racks and released their debut album, *Child Is Father to the Man*, in 1968, nearly a year before the Big Thing (eventually rechristened Chicago) made it to vinyl.

BS&T's first record, although embraced by rock critics, was only a moderate commercial success and yielded not a single hit. Kooper parted ways with this band, too. So did original members Randy Brecker and Jerry Weiss, both trumpet players.

It wasn't until the band reshuffled its lineup and added the burly David Clayton-Thomas as its lead singer that the public took notice. *Blood, Sweat and Tears*—with the top-ten hits "Spinning Wheel," "You've Made Me So Very Happy," and "And When I Die"—and *Blood, Sweat and Tears 3* both stayed at number one on the album charts for a stretch. But these albums were jazz-rock experimental to the point of excess. Variations of classical compositions by Bartok and Prokofiev were even added to a Steve Winwood song.

As for this baby genre called jazz-rock, the public turned its attention to the band Chicago, and Blood, Sweat and Tears took to the Las Vegas circuit.

CHICAGO

Blood, Sweat and Tears put the ball in play, but it was the seven-piece outfit called Chicago who scored goal after goal with a string of hit albums and singles in the jazz-rock mold.

What made Chicago the envy of music fans and especially students who played in school jazz-rock ensembles were three strong singer/songwriters: keyboardist Robert Lamm, bassist Peter Cetera, and guitar virtuoso Terry Kath, a Hendrix fan whose guitar prowess was overshadowed by the horn section. (Hendrix was a Kath fan in turn.)

First they called themselves the Big Thing, and played clubs throughout the Midwest. Producer James William Guercio, working with the Buckinghams at the time, caught a Big Thing gig in Niles, Michigan. After catching another show at Barnaby's, a Chicago nightspot, Guercio told the band to pack their bags and move to Los Angeles, where they lived and rehearsed in a small two-bedroom house beneath the Hollywood Freeway. Guercio renamed the band Chicago Transit Authority in honor of the bus line he rode as a kid. But after the release of their debut album in 1969, the band was forced to shorten their name to Chicago after litigation was threatened from the real Chicago Transit Authority.

No one ever accused Chicago of being overly creative with album titles. Until their twelfth release, *Hot Streets* (1978), each of their records bore a simple Roman numeral to designate its sequence in the Chicago catalog. But record buyers heard the creativity in the music. From 1970 to 1988, the band issued one top-twenty hit after another, most notably "25 or 6 to 4" (few fans caught the reference to a drug excursion in the wee hours), "Does Anybody

Chicago's "Ballet for a Girl in Buchanan," a seven-song suite, included the top-ten single "Make Me Smile" and the perennial prom theme "Colour My World." The suite put Chicago on the map.

Really Know What Time It Is?" "Saturday in the Park," "Feelin' Stronger Every Day," "Searchin' So Long," and "If You Leave Me Now." Chicago turned to disco-type pop in the eighties and, though the critics balked, enjoyed even greater success.

The turning point in the band's career, which led to the change toward a more pop, middle-of-the-road sound, was the tragic death of Terry Kath on January 23, 1978. A game of Russian roulette is often cited as the cause of his demise, but that's inaccurate. The truth is that Kath died while cleaning an automatic pistol, not a cylinder-loading gun commonly used for the fatal game.

The sole witness to the incident was Chicago keyboard technician Don Johnson. In the accompanying booklet to *Group Portrait*, Chicago's 1991 boxed set, Pankow relates Johnson's account of what happened: "He had the clip in one hand and the gun in the other, but evidently there was a bullet still in the chamber. He was waving the gun around his head. He said, 'What do you think I'm going to do? Blow my brains out?' And just the pressure of his finger on the trigger released that round in the chamber. It went into the side of his head. He died instantly. Only Terry knows what he was thinking at that moment." Whatever he was thinking was most likely clouded by drug use. "He was certainly more dependent on chemicals than he should have been," Pankow adds.

Chicago thought about dissolving after Kath's death, but the band soldiered on with replacement Donnie Dacus, followed by other personnel changes, and was a viable touring and recording entity into the nineties.

ELECTRIC LIGHT ORCHESTRA

The Electric Light Orchestra (ELO) wasn't the first rock band to tinker with orchestral string arrangements. The Moody Blues, Deep Purple, and, most notably, Procul Harum mixed violins with guitars. But the Electric Light Orchestra parlayed the rock-meets-classical recipe into an entire career, and enjoyed quite a successful run from 1971 until 1983.

Beatlemaniac Jeff Lynne had produced an album for the Idle Race, an obscure band, before joining British sensations the Move in 1970. The Move, past their prime by then, were a showcase for the bouncy-pop power of guitarist Roy Wood and drummer Bev Bevan, but after Lynne came aboard, their metamorphosis into the Electric Light Orchestra commenced. Adding session players and traditional classical instruments, they spent the better part of 1971 in a London studio assembling the first ELO album.

The Electric Light Orchestra rose from the ashes of the Move, who featured man-of-many-instruments Roy Wood (left). Keyboard player Richard Tandy (right) came aboard after the debut album was released.

That debut was released stateside in 1972 with the title *No Answer*. As the story goes, a United Artists record executive had his assistant call England to ask what the album's title would be. When the assistant wrote down "no answer," the exec took the message literally. ELO didn't take off in America until 1973, with their first U.S. tour and the release of their second album, *ELO II*, featuring the radio-friendly "Roll Over Beethoven." By the third record, *On the Third Day*, Lynne, always obsessed with studio wizardry, discovered ADT (automatic double tracking), which became an ELO hallmark on future hits "Evil Woman," "Telephone Line," and "Don't Bring Me Down."

ELO's stage shows became increasingly elaborate. In 1978, they played inside a replica of the monster spaceship that graced the cover of their 1977 release, *Out of the Blue*. "The flying saucer used to go down better than us some

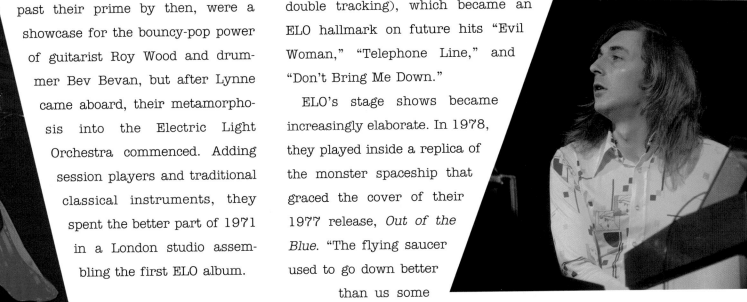

nights," Lynne joked to an interviewer. "It wasn't fun to play in." By 1983, with the release of *Secret Messages*, Lynne wasn't having any fun at all performing live with ELO. They released only one more album, *Balance of Power* (1986), and played a few reunion gigs that same year. Lynne's expertise as a master producer later resurfaced in records for George Harrison, Tom Petty, and the Traveling Wilburys.

EMERSON, LAKE AND PALMER

The keyboardist strapped himself to his piano bench and punished the ivories while the entire platform, grand piano and all, rotated until he was flailing away upside down. The drummer slammed and smacked his twenty-five-thousand-dollar percussion kit with reckless abandon as the whole shebang, including gong, xylophone, and timpani, ascended from the bandstand before exploding. And the guitarist, awash in lights, lasers, and smoke, strummed effortlessly and scored the band's biggest hits.

Emerson, Lake and Palmer (ELP) were as much fun to look at as to listen to. Although their ten albums retained the same art-rock-pop formula, their sold-out arena tours were the height of overkill, the epitome of the bombastic rock concert.

All three members held degrees in rock stardom before their first appearance together at the Isle of Wight Festival in 1970. Classically trained pianist Keith Emerson honed his keyboard antics in the Nice, a late-sixties classical-psychedelic outfit. (At one illustrious Nice concert at London's Royal Albert Hall, Emerson burned the American flag while playing Leonard Bernstein's "America" from *West Side Story*. Not surprisingly, they were banned from the hall.) Bassist Greg Lake was a founding member of King Crimson, but spent only a short period of time with Robert Fripp's audacious band. And drummer Carl Palmer played with the Crazy World of Arthur Brown, which scored a number two hit in 1968 with "Fire." (Brown, no stranger to stage antics himself,

Greg Lake (left) had been with King Crimson, Keith Emerson (center) had been with the Nice, and Carl Palmer (right) had done time with the Crazy World of Arthur Brown before the three coalesced.

finished his concerts by lighting what looked like his hair on fire. Actually, it was a steel helmet.)

The three-piece band might have been known as EBP—Emerson, Bachman and Palmer—had former Guess Who guitarist Randy Bachman been healthy enough to accept Emerson's invitation. But Emerson ended up teaming with Lake, and after efforts to snatch Mitch Mitchell from the Jimi Hendrix Experience fell through, destructo drummer Palmer signed on.

ELP's majestic songs, rife with images of knights in shining armor and other regal scenes, went on for full album sides, such as *Tarkus* (1971) and *Brain Salad Surgery* (1973). Lake was the romantic, and his compositions "Lucky Man" and "From the Beginning," although uncharacteristic of ELP's sonic boom, were hit singles and concert highlights. Their 1974 tour, their most ambitious, included thirty-six tons (32.6t) of equipment, not counting the fake snow that fell during the encore, "Silent Night."

A two-year hiatus that began in 1975 slowed the band's momentum. Their popularity waned considerably by 1977, when each member of the group had a solo side on the double set *Works*, appearing together for just the fourth side. When their 1978 release, *Love Beach*, failed to score with fans, ELP split up.

Solo careers took flight. Palmer helped form the art-rock retread Asia in 1981. An ELP reunion tour in 1993 brought the fans back to the arena for one last spectacle.

GENESIS

Genesis released so many smash hits in the eighties that it's easy to forget that they honed their craft as a theatrical-art group in the late sixties.

The band didn't play its first rehearsal with ideas of fancy costumes and smoke-filled stages. Garden Wall was the name of a songwriter's club formed in 1966 by four ambitious lads from the British secondary school Charterhouse. Tony Banks, Peter Gabriel, Anthony Phillips, and Michael Rutherford penned a pile of songs that they played for anyone who would listen before Jonathan King—a producer and performer who had scored an American hit in 1965 with "Everyone's Gone to the Moon"—was moved by a demo tape to call them up in 1968. With promises of a recording contract and a suggestion that they call themselves Genesis, he ushered the four into a studio, where they cut their first single, the uneventful "The Silent Sun," and their first album, *From Genesis to Revelation*.

Two drummers came and went before Phil Collins signed on. With the addition of Steve Hackett on guitar, the first stable lineup of Genesis was intact for the recording of the second album, *Trespass*. But the band attracted only a cult following before their 1972 release, *Foxtrot*. That year, they played their first concert date in the United States, at Brandeis University in Massachusetts.

Phil Collins (above) became Genesis' lead singer after Peter Gabriel embarked on a solo career in 1975. Collins' voice approximated the sound of Peter Gabriel's, and he'd already sung lead for the band on a 1973 song.

In performance, the Genesis of the early seventies was a showcase for Gabriel and his cast of costumed, peculiar characters. He was a giant sunflower for "Willow Farm," and a mysterious space being for "Watcher of the Skies," and an ornery codger for "Musical Box." In 1975, Gabriel, longing to expand as an artist, shocked the rock world with the announcement of his departure from Genesis. A search for his replacement was begun.

An endless series of contenders were auditioned, but Genesis finally settled on the guy who had sung lead on "More Fool Me" from their 1973 disc *Selling England by the Pound*, their own drummer, Phil Collins. He didn't sound very different from Gabriel, and in concert, Collins would stray from the drums to sing front and center as a relief drummer rushed on. For the first tour, it was former Yes trapsman Bill Bruford.

Gone were the odd works on which Genesis had built its foundation. With Collins up front, shorter songs took hold. Live, the band retained its visual edge the best it could, with an elaborate light show and dry-ice fog. *A Trick of the Tail*, released in 1976, was their first album without Gabriel. By 1978, Hackett was history as well. Genesis recorded the appropriately titled *...And Then There Were Three*, which included their first U.S. single, the upbeat "Follow You, Follow Me," and set the stage for a slew of gold albums and hit singles that would continue well into the eighties. By 1981, Collins had launched his own solo career, which, on a commercial level, eclipsed Gabriel's.

JETHRO TULL

There was no one named Jethro in Jethro Tull, but there was someone to watch and marvel at in leader Ian Anderson, whom audiences loved for his furious flute playing and demented stage antics. As for the music, rock plus classical plus folk plus jazz equals Tull.

Anderson had been the lead singer in John Evan's Smash, a six-piece British pub band that dissolved after only one unfruitful year on the circuit. With Smash holdover Glenn Cornick at his side, Anderson enlisted the services of singer/guitarist Mick Abrahams and drummer Clive Bunker, and they took the name of Jethro Tull, an eighteenth-century agriculturist and inventor of the seed drill. A first single, "Aeroplane" backed with "Sunshine Day," was committed to tape, but a funny thing happened on the way to the record plant. Their name was misprinted on the label as Jethro Toe. Just as well. This "Aeroplane" never took off.

Anderson concentrated on his flute playing. He perfected the techniques of flutter-tonguing and singing through the flute by listening to Rahsaan Roland Kirk albums for hours. Soon Anderson was the star of the show, and Abrahams left to form Blodwyn Pig following the release of Jethro Tull's debut album, *This Was*, and was replaced by Martin Barre.

Their next single, "Living in the Past," became their biggest hit in the States several years later. With the release of the multiplatinum *Aqualung* (1972), their stardom was cemented. Tours for this must-see band sold out quickly, and progressive FM radio made a home for the title track and two other songs, "Cross-Eyed Mary" and "Locomotive Breath."

Bunker was replaced by Barriemore Barlow, and Tull grew even more adventurous with

Woodwind wizard Ian Anderson danced about the stage like a leprechaun on speed, and gave Jethro Tull fans something to look at as well as listen to. Anderson's unkempt hair and beard and his propensity for wearing the traditional tartan-plaid on stage only added to his mystique.

Thick as a Brick. The title track was the sole track and stretched for two sides through various themes. The album, packaged as a newspaper, hit number one in America.

A Passion Play (1973) was dismissed by once-enthusiastic critics as self-indulgent rubbish. Feeling the heat, Anderson and Tull took a two-year hiatus from performing. *War Child* (1974) boasted their second U.S. single in "Bungle in the Jungle," and then Tull's lineup shuffled yet again for one of classic rock's most memorable album titles, *Too Old to Rock 'n' Roll, Too Young to Die.* Several more releases—Tull's deepest excursions into traditional folk—followed before the band closed out the decade with *Storm Watch.*

More albums followed in the eighties, most notably *Broadsword and the Beat* (1982) and *Crest of a Knave* (1987). Although the record racks are stuffed with more than one Jethro Tull greatest-hits package, a boxed set issued in 1993 commemorating their twenty-fifth anniversary neatly summed up their eccentric legacy.

THE MOODY BLUES

The Moody Blues would have been showcased in the "British Invasion" chapter of this book had Denny Laine stayed on instead of leaving in 1967. (Eventually, the singer/guitarist teamed with Paul McCartney and Wings.) Perhaps Laine would have steered the Moodies along the path they originally carved in 1965 when their single "Go Now" went top ten.

But singer/guitarist Justin Hayward and bassist John Lodge had more grandiose ideas when they picked up the slack left by Laine and original bassist Clint Warwick. *Days of Future Passed*, recorded with the London Festival Orchestra and sprung on an unsuspecting public in 1967, became a classic rock masterpiece and served as a blueprint for many classical-rock acts to follow.

Looking back, the Moody Blues repertoire seems pompous and overblown. But in 1967, concept albums like the Beatles' *Sgt. Pepper's Lonely Hearts Club Band* were just coming into vogue. Along with Procul Harum, whose "A Whiter Shade of Pale" was released that same summer, the Moody Blues were hailed as fresh and exciting. Although the song "Nights in White Satin" was included on *Days*, the single didn't become a hit in America until 1972, when the album went back up the charts and into gold status. No one knows what prompted the Moodies to wed rock with classical music. Maybe the notion struck

The Moody Blues' 1965 hit, "Go Now," with its big Merseybeat sound, had little in common with the classical-rock direction the band headed in after singer/guitarist Denny Laine split in 1967.

one night at the LSD parties they allegedly threw with Pete Townshend, Ginger Baker, and assorted glitterati in attendance, according to the British tabloid *News of the World*.

After *Days*, the Moodies refused to stray from the classical-rock-bombast course, and album after album repeated the same formula until it became hackneyed: straight-face spoken word introductions, hot-air prose and poetry, lush orchestral passages provided by a real orchestra or a Mellotron, and lots of three-part harmonies. And there was some rock and roll in there, too.

Amazingly, even their singles struck gold. "Tuesday Afternoon (Forever Afternoon)" is still in heavy rotation on many classic rock stations, as is "I'm Just a Singer (in a Rock and Roll Band)." But the Moodies ran out of steam in the mid-seventies and the members detoured into solo waters. They re-formed in 1978 for their eighth album, appropriately titled *Octave*, and now synthesizers were part of the plan. Original keyboardist Mike Pinder eventually threw in the towel and in came Patrick Moraz, a former member of Yes. The Moodies assumed yet another incarnation and took *Long Distance Voyager* all the way to number one in 1981. A tour followed, their first in years. By that time, critics were fully revolted, but that didn't stop Moraz and company from soldiering on through the eighties with a slew of moderately successful titles.

QUEEN

"I like the cabaret-ish sort of thing," Freddie Mercury told *Circus* magazine in 1977. "I absolutely adore Liza Minelli, she's a total wow. The way she delivers her songs—the sheer energy. The way the lights enhance every movement of the show. I think you can see similarities in the excitement and energy of a Queen show. It's not glam rock, you see. We're in the show business tradition."

Was it cabaret or rock and roll? An arena ruckus or Vegas kitsch? With the flamboyant Freddie Mercury at the helm, it was both. Queen, the masters of opera rock, were also masters of excess. "The Cecil B. DeMille of Rock" was Mercury's way of putting it. And not only on the concert stage; their after-show soirees, too, were notoriously big-budget extravaganzas replete with mud wrestlers and circus midgets. As for the records, call it the sound of a zillion overdubs.

Ask any hard rocker of the eighties or nineties about his inspiration, and four out of five will inevitably answer with the same two groups: Kiss and Queen. But where Kiss spit fire and loaded on gobs of garish greasepaint, Queen's act was a bit more refined, showcasing both a twenty-six-foot (7.9m) -high crown as a stage setting and a vaudevillian ham, lead singer Mercury. And Kiss's guitarist, Paul Stanley, was no match for the ax acrobatics of Queen's Brian May.

Mercury, born in Zanzibar, Africa, reared in India, and schooled at London's Ealing College of Art (he was a graphic-design major), was going nowhere with a band called Wreckage. He recorded under the name Larry Lurex, too, but that character went belly-up as well. Same for guitarist May and drummer Roger Taylor, whose talents in a college quartet called Smile were going similarly unnoticed. When Smile's sole single,

Freddie Mercury—an over-the-top performer in the grand show business tradition.

"Earth," failed to make the charts, the band folded. May and Taylor merged with Mercury for a group called Queen, a name Mercury had conjured up years earlier. John Deacon answered a classified ad and was hired, and the band began two years of writing and recording for what would become their debut album, *Queen*.

American fans didn't bow down to Queen, though, until the band's third album, *Sheer Heart Attack*, and the single that eventually went top-twenty stateside, "Killer Queen." Critics called it hogwash, and likened the band's sound to Beach Boys harmonies trapped in Led Zeppelin raunch. Mercury's response? "Robert Plant is my favorite singer. And he actually said he liked 'Killer Queen.'"

The Queen formula came to fruition in 1975 with the release of *A Night at the Opera*, an album that cost a lot to produce but was worth every penny. The album's centerpiece, the mock-operatic assemblage "Bohemian Rhapsody," shot to the top ten on the strength of Brian May's soaring, helium-filled guitar lines and Mercury's overdubs. For some reason, the band took pride in eschewing electronic keyboards and printed the disclaimer "No synthesizers!" in *Opera*'s liner notes. The Marx Brothers would have been proud of Queen's next album title, *A Day at the Races*, which included the top-twenty hit "Somebody to Love."

Freddie Mercury (left, with John Deacon, center, and Brian May) laid down dozens of vocal tracks for the six-minute "Bohemian Rhapsody," Queen's first U.S. hit.

Queen's 1977 opus, *News of the World* (why not *Duck Soup*?), went platinum, boosted by the double A-side coupling of May's "We Will Rock You" with Mercury's "We Are the Champions." But it wasn't until Queen abandoned the operatics and went with a more disco-type approach on *The Game* (1980) that the band zoomed to the top of both the album and singles charts. "Another One Bites the Dust" might have repulsed diehard Queenheads with its tedious beat, but it won over many new fans, who went equally gaga over the rockabilly-flavored "Crazy Little Thing Called Love." Mercury's new look didn't sit well with the loyal devotees, either. Close-cropped hair and a thick black mustache seemed more akin to the Village People than the Zeppelinesque rock the band had peddled years earlier.

A 1981 duet with David Bowie, "Under Pressure," was also disco fodder, but the members of the band were still, and to the end, heroes in their native England. Their 1986 jaunt played to a record 400,000 fans—150,000 alone for a two-night stand at Wembley Arena—and boasted the largest lighting apparatus and stage set ever assembled for a rock concert. Sadly, it was Queen's final tour, as Mercury was diagnosed with AIDS soon afterward. He was highly secretive about his condition, and spent time only with close friends during his last three years at his flat in London's Earl's Court. On November 24, 1991, at the age of forty-five, Freddie Mercury became the first major rock star known to succumb to the AIDS virus.

RUSH

Say an unkind word about this Canadian trio of virtuosos and prepare to have your head handed to you. Through twenty-one years and seventeen albums, Rush has maintained one of rock's most loyal followings. For devotees, this isn't rock, it's a religion.

Complex rhythms, difficult time changes, spotlight solos, and Geddy Lee's banshee wail are what brings fans back for more year after year. Originally launched in Toronto as a bar band, playing sci-fi heavy metal with Lee on bass, Alex Lifeson on guitar, and John Rutsey on drums, Rush sharpened its man-against-technology music all through the seventies. Rutsey was replaced with Neil Peart after the release of *Rush* (1974), and Peart's lyric-writing ability was put to good, if a bit bloated, use. "Cygnus X-1" told the story of a spaceship plung-

Since their inception in 1969, Canadian trio Rush (which includes guitarist Alex Lifeson, left, with singer/bassist Geddy Lee) has built a deeply committed fan base along the lines of the Grateful Dead.

ing through a black hole. The entire first side of *2112*, released in 1976 and inspired by an Ayn Rand novel, dealt with a boy who finds an electric guitar and is subsequently chased by the law for inventing rock music. As you can imagine, critics had a field day deriding Rush's histrionics.

Rush became more radio-friendly in the eighties with the release of *Permanent Waves* (1980) and *Moving Pictures* (1981). Songs like "Limelight" and "Tom Sawyer" were scaled-down singles in comparison with the mammoth earlier works. These tunes, along with "Time Stand Still," "Free Will," and "Closer to the Heart" remain concert staples to this day, and that probably explains Rush's massive appeal. Like AC/DC, Kiss, and Ozzy Osbourne, Rush gives the fans what they want, tour after sold-out tour, no questions asked.

YES

It didn't matter that the critics said no. Yes, a troupe of classically trained musicians, was the preeminent progressive rock band. Yes didn't write songs; they composed suites, catchy, harmony-heavy suites set to keyboard-based classical rock. Seventeen albums worth, many of them megasellers. Fans couldn't get enough.

Those fans would never have heard radio regulars like "Roundabout" and "All Good People" had singer Jon Anderson not struck up a friendship with bassist Chris Squire one night in May 1968 over drinks at a small London nightclub called La Chasse. Soon they recruited guitarist Peter Banks, drummer Bill Bruford, and keyboardist Tony Kaye, and settled on the name Yes.

The first Yes gig was played at the East Mersey Youth Camp, followed by a string of dates at London's Marquee club. Then, on one fateful evening, the five members of Yes were shaken from their sleep and asked to sit in for Sly and the Family Stone, who had failed to show for a gig at Blaise's, a popular nightspot. The audience, though anticipating an evening of funk, went head over heels over this new group, and the word was out. An opening stint at Cream's farewell concert at the Royal Albert Hall intensified the buzz.

Their self-titled first album won a big audience in England, mixing original compositions with cover tunes, but their second release, *Time and a Word*, did little to advance their careers.

By the third release, Banks had handed in his resignation so that he could form Flash; Steve Howe filled his shoes quite admirably. His compositions were the catalyst for *The Yes Album* (1971) and the FM standards "Your Move/All Good People," "Starship Trooper," and "Yours Is No Disgrace."

Tony Kaye was the next to leave (to form Badger), and in waltzed keyboard killer Rick Wakeman, who had done time with the Strawbs. Now the classic Yes lineup was intact—Wakeman, Bruford, Howe, Squire, and Anderson—and the two albums they recorded together, *Fragile* and

Yes first hit it big in Britain, where they were celebrated as a supergroup even before the release of their first album.

Close to the Edge, are regarded by disciples as Yes' finest. A triple-disc live album, *Yessongs*, came next.

Bruford was Yes history by 1972, and he joined King Crimson. Alan White took his place, and this new grouping set out on Yes' most ambitious work to date, *Tales of Topographic Oceans*, a decent-selling double set based on the Buddhist Shastic Scriptures. Rock critics would have nothing to do with it, and blasted *Tales* as ponderous and messy drivel.

Wakeman cried "uncle" and left to record on his own. Film composer Patrick Moraz (formerly of Refugee and future member of the Moody Blues) signed on with Yes, and 1974 brought *Relayer*, which returned to the tried-and-true formula of one side-long suite backed with two ten-minute epics. The compilation *Yesterdays* came next.

Then Wakeman returned for *Going for the One* (1977) and *Tormato* (1978). Wakeman left yet again, this time followed by Anderson, their primary lyricist for all these years. Their odd replacements, Geoff Downes and Trevor Horn from the Buggles, a new-wave band, could do little to save *Drama* (1980). Yes broke up, but not for good.

Anderson returned through the famous Yes revolving door, and the band scored a second wind with *90125* (1983), including the return-to-form "Owner of a Lonely Heart," which incorporated a bit of technology unavailable to the band in those early years. Fans and the uninitiated searching for one solid package that ties the entire Yes story together should investigate *Yesyears* (1991), a four-CD set.

FRANK ZAPPA

You'll rarely hear a Frank Zappa song on classic rock radio, but the late bandleader/guitarist/singer/songwriter/producer/you-name-it deserves mention in a book about the music he based his enigmatic career on. Zappa's fan base and influence are immeasurable. He never forgot that rock was essentially for kids, and his catalog of nearly fifty recordings features complex and sometimes reckless arrangements, adolescent humor, biting satire, a fair share of gross-outs, and a relentless penchant for weirdness.

He certainly exceeded the boundaries of rock, incorporating jazz, avant-garde, blues, classical, and even doo-wop into his art. Born Francis Vincent Zappa, Jr., on December 21, 1940, in Baltimore, Maryland, Zappa and his family moved to California while he was still in elementary school. He developed a love not only for fifties doo-wop and rhythm and blues, but for modern classical composers as well; later in his career, he told interviewers that Edgard Varèse was a key influence.

A nervous MGM Records tagged the words "of Invention" onto the name of his first major band, the Mothers, and in 1966, Zappa embarked on a busy recording career with *Freak Out!* The Mothers toured endlessly, and personnel changed constantly with noted jazz musicians like Jean-Luc Ponty and George Duke, fellow Zappa eccentric Captain Beefheart (Don Van Vliet), and even former Turtles Mark Volman and Howard Kaylan serving time at one point or another. But for all of Zappa's albums—most notably *We're Only in It for the Money* (1967), *Uncle Meat* (1969), *Hot Rats* (1970), *Overnite Sensation* (1973), *One Size Fits All* (1975), *Sheik Yerbouti* (1979), the *Shut Up 'n Play Yer Guitar* series of the early eighties, and the

You Can't Do That on Stage Anymore CDs of the late eighties—Zappa rarely sold huge numbers of records. His only top-forty single was the insipid "Valley Girl," recorded with his daughter, Moon Unit. Another commercial success was "Dancin' Fool" (1979), the ultimate antidisco song.

In the eighties, Zappa crusaded for the First Amendment and appeared at congressional hearings to denounce censorship and the formation of the Parents Music Resource Center (PMRC), a group determined to remedy the objectionable lyrics in rock. "Ladies, we are treating dandruff with decapitation," was his oft-quoted line. He continued to record into the early nineties, but was forced to cut back considerably on his workload when he began to lose his long battle with prostate cancer. Zappa died at his home in Los Angeles on December 4, 1993, surrounded by his wife, Gail, daughter Moon Unit, and sons Dweezil and Ahmet.

Frank Zappa (seated right, with one of the many incarnations of the Mothers of Invention) was a rocker with powerful cult appeal. Among his many projects was research into an eighteenth-century composer named Francesco Zappa, whose work he recorded on a synthesizer.

THE FASHION PLATES

By the end of the sixties, more and more inhibitions were evaporating as rock grew louder and even more adventurous, and kids took their fashion cue from rock stars. Hair grew longer, wardrobes became flashier, and the catch phrases of the day, "If it feels good, do it," "Let it all hang out," and "Let it be" were splattered over posters, buttons, and T-shirts.

New technologies were advancing at breakneck speeds. After astronaut Neil Armstrong walked on the moon on July 20, 1969, David Bowie penned the words to "Space Oddity." Three years later, Bowie took on the persona of space android Ziggy Stardust in recordings and concerts. Space talk and eerie messages began to creep into records by Pink Floyd as early as 1968. Their second album, *A Saucerful of Secrets*, included the legendary "Set the Controls for the Heart of the Sun." Floyd's 1969 double set, *Ummagumma*, was progressive space-rock at its most indulgent. Even Steve Miller sang about a "Space Cowboy" on his 1969 LP, *Brave New World*. And wasn't that some sort of futuristic airplane the topless girl was holding on the cover of *Blind Faith*?

David Bowie was more than a spaceman, though. His androgynous spin on the whole rock affair put his sexuality into question and kicked off the era of glam rock, also called glitter rock. In 1969, the gay liberation movement was just picking up steam. After a Christopher Street bar in Greenwich Village was raided by police, a protest march, later to be called the Stonewall revolution, rallied gays together across New York City, and across America as well. You didn't have to be gay to love Bowie, of coarse. Millions of kids were moonstruck by his talents.

David Bowie; Marc Bolan of T. Rex; Sweet's Andy Scott.

At a Radio City Music Hall concert in February 1973, one overzealous male fan knocked the wind out of Bowie after jumping on stage and planting a wet smooch on his lips.

Sequined outfits, platform shoes, mascara, rouge, eyeliner—in came the glammers. Plenty of guys moussed up their hair and squeezed into spandex outfits two sizes too small. The music might have played second fiddle to the cosmetics, but that was all part of the fun. For the most part, glam rock was the same old song, all dressed up. John Lennon probably said it best: "It's great, you know, but it's just rock and roll with lipstick on."

DAVID BOWIE

A job résumé should be only one page long, but if you're David Bowie, you'll need several more sheets of paper. Here goes: singer/songwriter/producer/saxophonist/pianist/guitarist/film actor/stage thespian/pantomime/painter/fashion plate/New Wave father figure—and we've only just begun. Always one step ahead of his contemporaries, Bowie continually reinvented and revitalized his music and his image during the classic rock years. In retrospect, he may have been the most important rock figure of the seventies. He definitely was the first to present a fictional rockstar persona, via Ziggy Stardust.

Born David Robert Jones, Bowie adopted the name of the hunting knife to avoid confusion with the Monkees' Davy Jones. Would anyone have mixed up the two?

Born David Robert Jones on January 8, 1947, Bowie grew up in London's Bromley and Brixton districts, and distinctly remembers being floored by the rhythm and blues and rock and roll shows he caught at nightspots like the Scene, the Marquee, and Eel Pie Island in

Twickenham. Little Richard's flamboyance influenced young Jones as much as Anthony Newley's crooning did. An avid record collector and voracious reader—in his teens, he was consumed with Kerouac, Kafka, and Isherwood—Jones was a shy and withdrawn only child, but found a bigger family in music and bohemian life.

By age thirteen, Jones was playing a saxophone that his dad, a publicist for a children's home, had purchased, and was in his first band, the Konrads, while still a student at Bromley Technical School. Here he befriended young Peter Frampton and a boy named George Underwood, who figures prominently in the Jones/Bowie bio. It was Underwood who punched Jones in the eye one day, landing him in the hospital for three months. Following surgery, the pupil of his left eye was paralyzed.

David Jones wanted to be either a painter, a musician, or an advertising agency staffer, and upon graduation, the third was his immediate choice. In due time, the music bug took hold, and holding no grudges, he and Underwood formed the King Bees. After stints with cover bands called the Lower Third and the Manish Boys (Jimmy Page played guitar on a studio session or two), David Jones changed his name to David Bowie, after the Bowie knife, to avoid confusion with the Monkee who shared his name.

Bowie recorded his first solo singles for Pye Records (1965)—including the very first song he remembers writing, the wistful "Can't Help Thinking About Me"—before spending time in a Buddhist monastery in Scotland as well as apprenticing in Lindsay Kemp's Underground Mime Troupe. Kemp had a huge influence on Bowie, and the decadent lifestyle he became accustomed to during this period was translated into the songs of his first album, *The World of David Bowie* (1967), released by Deram, a British label. In interviews, Bowie likened his sound to a baroque Anthony Newley.

In 1969, after appearing in low-budget art films, some of which he'd never even see, Bowie formed the Beckenham Arts lab, an experimental music, film, poetry, and theater conclave, and wrote "Space Oddity" after astronaut Neil Armstrong walked on the moon. A record deal with Mercury resulted in *Man of Words, Man*

David Bowie reinvented his persona again and again during the classic rock period. By the nineties, he had settled down to a more select and comfortable diet of standard rock fare.

of Music, sounding more folk than rock, and a disastrous supporting tour during the first skinhead movement of 1969. Bowie was besieged by spitting and cigarette butts. This, years ahead of the punk movement.

With *The Man Who Sold the World* (1970), guitarist Mick Ronson and bassist Tony Visconti (later to produce Bowie and

CLASSIC ROCK

many others) came aboard, and Bowie entered a period of electric guitar rock, sidestepping just a bit for a tribute to New York City, an album called *Hunky Dory* (1971). In 1972, the fictional rock character Ziggy Stardust was brought to life in Bowie's watershed, *The Rise and Fall of Ziggy Stardust and the Spiders from Mars*. The attendant road tour presented Bowie as Ziggy, an android from another world who touched down onstage in his own glass-domed spaceship, replete with futuristic costumes, extravagant makeup, and spiked orange hair. The album and tour catapulted Bowie to rock star status.

This was glitter rock at its height, and audiences in London and New York went gaga. After the follow-up, the equally surreal *Aladdin Sane* (1973), Bowie took a break to produce records for Lou Reed (*Transformer*, including "Walk on the Wild Side") and Mott the Hoople (*All the Young Dudes*, for which Bowie also wrote the title track; they rejected "Suffragette City," which he initially offered). He also mixed *Raw Power* for friend Iggy Pop.

A cover album of sixties British rock, *Pin-Ups* (1974), was next, followed by more sci-fi rock, a bit more pompous, in *Diamond Dogs*, and a double live album, *David Live*, recorded at Philadelphia's Tower Theatre. *Young Americans* (1975) offered more Philadelphia soul, and his first number one single, "Fame," cowritten with John Lennon, was committed to tape in a single evening session.

For all his success, Bowie was uncertain of his identity. He'd hidden behind so many characters—Ziggy, Aladdin Sane, and the Thin White Duke, each with his own personality and environment—that an identity crisis was inevitable. After starring in Nicolas Roeg's *The Man Who Fell to Earth* (1976), Bowie holed up in a Los Angeles house and was, as he told rock chronicler Timothy White in the book *Rock Lives*, "totally washed up emotionally and physically, completely screwed up."

Bowie escaped to Berlin in 1977 and entered into a period of electronic music assisted by Brian Eno. *Low*, *"Heroes,"* and *Lodger*, the first two albums more ethereal and experimental than the third, serve as a Bowie-Eno trilogy with guest appearances by guitarist Robert Fripp.

Bowie moved to New York in 1979 to record *Scary Monsters*, a culmination of all his styles. The album included two staples of classic rock radio, "Ashes to Ashes" and "Fashion."

What was left to conquer? How about the Broadway stage? His portrayal of the title role in *The Elephant Man* won decent reviews, leading to major roles in two movies, *Merry Christmas, Mr. Lawrence* and *The Hunger*. Bowie continued recording through the eighties, both solo (*Let's Dance* was an international smash in 1983) and with Tin Machine, a bland four-piece band, which included the sons of television comedian Soupy Sales.

MOTT THE HOOPLE

Name the glam rock band originally influenced by Bob Dylan and (dare I say it?) Sonny Bono. Here's a clue: they nearly packed it in after four albums before being rescued by fellow glitter rocker David Bowie. Need another hint? Their colorful front man was rarely seen without his trademark sunglasses. Those who answered Mott the Hoople win a lovely pair of platform shoes with ten-inch (25.4cm) stacked heels dipped in silver glitter.

Island Records A&R executive Guy Stevens loved everything about a band called Silence except the singer, Stan Tippens. Guitarist Mick Ralphs, organist Verden Allen, and the others were all fine, but Tippens had to go. Ian Hunter, who had played bass with Freddie "Fingers" Lee and Billy Fury, had been reduced to making demos at night while working in a factory by day. After Hunter played "Like a Rolling Stone" and Bono's "Laugh at Me" at his audition for Silence, he was in. Tippens took a lesser role: road manager.

Renaming themselves after an 1849 Willard Manus novel that Stevens had read while in jail, Mott the Hoople cut their self-titled debut in 1969. Hunter sang with a Dylanesque rasp, and the entire album was easily compared to Dylan's *Blonde on Blonde*. Hunter's Sonny Bono song made the cut, as did an instrumental version of the Kinks' "You Really Got Me," but it was "Rock and Roll Queen" that stood out, and Mott the Hoople was immediately booked into nightclubs. Their very first gig at the Batman Cavern Club in Riccone, Italy, led to their debut in England at the Abernale Youth Club, and the band was soon courting a rabid following. "You Really Got Me" would stretch for twenty minutes, and "Rock and Roll Queen" was a showstopper. Hunter, playing piano at the time, would get so worked up he'd kick over the keyboards, just as his idol Jerry Lee Lewis had in his heyday. (In 1971, Mott was banned from London's Albert Hall after enraptured fans ripped apart dozens of seats.)

By 1970, during American and British tours with Free, Traffic, Mountain, and Jethro Tull, Anderson was playing guitar and trading licks, the spotlight, and tense moments with Ralphs. But Mott the Hoople albums sold poorly. After *Mad Shadows* (1970), *Wildlife* (1971), and *Brain Capers* (1971) failed to set sales records, the band nearly folded. In the liner notes to *The Ballad of Mott*, a retrospective released in 1993, Hunter laments, "We were playing in Zurich in a gas tank that had been converted into a club, and we thought, 'If this is fame, forget it.'" This low point of their career was documented on "The Ballad of Mott the Hoople" from the *Mott* album (1973).

When David Bowie caught wind of the band's frustrations, he agreed to supply them with a song. But Hunter thought "Suffragette City," which Bowie first offered, wasn't good enough.

Even when Mott the Hoople's unmistakable Ian Hunter (left, with Ariel Bender) wanted to remove his trademark sunglasses, the band insisted that they stay on.

After Bowie sat on the floor with a guitar and played "All the Young Dudes," Hunter knew it was the hit they wanted. "Dudes" became Mott's only top-forty single in America, the title track of their fifth album, their first for Columbia Records. Bowie ended up producing the entire two sides, including a version of Lou Reed's "Sweet Jane," and teaching the band a few things about working in the studio. He also told Hunter that if the band were to survive, Hunter should take sole charge, a bit of advice that didn't sit well with Ralphs.

The U.S. tour in late 1972 showcased a new Mott in full glitter rock regalia, with sequined costumes, rhinestones, mascara, and platform heels amid the heavy camp. "We became instant queers," Hunter wrote in his journal of the tour, *Reflections of a Rock Star*. "Of course, we weren't. It was all very funny." The band's follow-ups were just as strong as the Bowie project, *Mott* (featuring "All the Way to Memphis"), and *The Hoople* (1974). But tensions came to a head during the production of *Mott*. A fight between Hunter and Ralphs during the mixing of the song "Violence" led to Ralphs' departure. Luther Grosvenor, from Spooky Tooth, changed his name to Ariel Bender and signed up. Ralphs hooked up with singer Paul Rodgers and formed Bad Company.

In 1974, Mott the Hoople became the first rock band to play a Broadway stage. Their one-week engagement at the Uris Theatre, with Queen opening, was captured on one side of Mott's 1974 *Live* album; a London concert appeared on the flip. Next came the addition of Mick Ronson, who replaced Bender, but that move ended up breaking up the band. The rest of the group grew intensely jealous of the attention the new guitarist received. After a European tour and an appearance on *Top of the Pops*, Ronson announced his departure, as did Hunter, following a stay at a New Jersey hospital for nervous exhaustion. Mott the Hoople had run its course.

SLADE

While America ignored them, Britain adored them. Between 1971 and 1974, Slade racked up twelve top-five singles in the U.K., six of them number one hits, and left concert halls in shambles with a garish stage act. It would take a short-lived American heavy metal band called Quiet Riot—who rerecorded Slade's "Cum on Feel the Noize" note-for-note to massive acceptance in 1983—to finally bring Slade decent recognition in the States.

Slade didn't begin as a glam rock band. Calling themselves N' Betweens, and later Ambrose Slade, their initial look was close-cut haircuts, blue jeans, and work boots. The skinheads, naturally, loved them. So did Chas Chandler, the former Animal, who agreed to manage them. Dropping

Slade showed a love for glamming and phonetically spelled song titles like "Skweeze Me Pleeze Me."

the Ambrose from their name, Chandler steered Slade onto the proper course and had them cutting hit singles in no time.

As their luck changed, so did their image. Singer Noddy Holder took to wearing oversize hats, flashy suspenders, and three different shades of plaid all at once. Guitarist Dave Hill cut the perfect glitter-rock image in knee-high boots with skyscraper heels and spangled hair. Concerts became exercises in excess, with brassieres and empty bottles littering the bandstand before the encores. Slade's song titles were as dumb as the look: "Look Wot You Dun" and "Mama Weer All Crazee Now" just a sample.

SWEET

Throw the 1910 Fruitgum Company and Led Zeppelin into a Cuisinart and what do you get? Try Sweet, whose batch of catchier-than-Velcro, pop-rock-glam songs won the hearts of pimply preteens while irritating the bejesus out of "serious" rock fans.

Singer Brian Connelly and drummer Mick Tucker formed the band in 1968. As Wainwright's Gentlemen, they were nothing more than a Motown and psychedelic cover band, but once the producing-songwriting team of Nicky Chinn and Mike Chapman got hold of them, the whole ball of wax turned sticky sweet. "Funny Funny," "Co-Co," and "Wig-Wam Bam" were part of a nearly unbroken string of U.K. hits before the band mixed in a dose of predated cock-rock for "Little Willy," their first U.S. hit, then

turned up the volume for *Desolation Boulevard.* "Ballroom Blitz" and "Fox on the Run," both from that 1975 album, made the top five on the U.S. singles charts.

The band members grew tired of their Bazooka image and even badmouthed Chinn and Chapman to the press after severing ties later in the decade. "Every time they heard something raw, they'd sprinkle fairy dust on it," bassist Steve Priest complained to an interviewer. But without Chinn and Chapman (who, a decade later, injected his pop-production prowess into hits for Blondie and the Knack), Sweet turned sour. Granted, their "Love Is Like Oxygen" went top-ten in 1978, but after that, a thousand tanks of helium couldn't lift their pop-metal off the ground.

T. REX

If anyone deserves to be crowned King of Glam Rock, it's Marc Bolan. Bolan *was* T. Rex. While Bowie outgrew the genre, and Gary Glitter's paunch cast him as a cross between Liberace and Benny Hill, Bolan was the ultimate glamster. Boyishly handsome with a strong jawline, eyes like saucers, floppy curls, and a sultry baritone voice, no one looked better in a hooded cape, mohair jacket, and Abe Lincoln stovepipe hat than Bolan.

Bolan's particular brand of flower-power glam was steeped in whimsical mythology and conjured up images of elves, unicorns, wizards, and sorcerers. Offstage, the singer was a family man, and although he would try anything once, he shunned pharmaceuticals and touched nothing stronger than a glass of wine. When he died in 1977, he was elevated to legend status.

Born Mark Feld on September 30, 1947, in the London suburb of Hackney, Bolan won a job modeling suits before he snagged a record deal with the Decca label at age eighteen. He was chagrined to see the acetate of his first single, "The Wizard," credited to Marc Bowland, which Decca thought was a more appealing name than Mark Feld. After some bickering, both parties agreed on Marc Bolan.

Solo singles for Decca went nowhere, but did lead him into the pioneering glam-rock band John's Children, who had a hit with the Bolan-penned "Desdemona." Onstage, Bolan was already perfecting his visuals. At one point in the show, he brought out a chain whip and assaulted his guitar, then tied up the speakers with chains and dragged them across the stage. By 1967, he was out of the band.

Steve Peregrine Took was the name of Bolan's first ally in Tyrannosaurus Rex. With Bolan on acoustic guitar and Took on bongos, Rex's first

Marc Bolan (above) called his act Tyrannosaurus Rex until 1970 and his departure with Steve Peregrine Took. With drummer Mickey Finn, Bolan and T. Rex scored biggest in the U.S. with "Bang a Gong (Get It On)" in 1972.

incarnation was as an eccentric, psychedelic-acoustic hybrid. Their album titles were just as lofty as the music inside: *My People Were Fair and Had Sky in Their Hair But Now They're Content to Wear Stars on Their Brows* (1968) was followed by *Prophets, Seers, and Sages: The Angels of the Ages* (1968) and *Unicorn* (1969) before Took, who was dropping acid on a daily basis, bid Bolan adieu. (Took choked to death on a cocktail cherry on October 27, 1980.)

Bolan returned with drummer Mickey Finn, shortened the handle to T. Rex, and brought his electric guitars out of hiding for a new glam approach and a string of seven British albums, the most notable being *Electric Warrior* (1971). But like his fellow glam purveyors, Bolan was never as successful in the U.S. as he was in the U.K., and "Bang a Gong (Get It On)" was his sole hit in the States. Years later, only progressive radio found a home for "Telegram Sam," "Jeepster," and "Metal Guru," catchy hard-rock glam stompers owing a bit to fifties rockabilly.

Bolan's star waned through the mid-seventies. In 1975, thoroughly discouraged, he left his wife, broke up with Finn, and flew to America, where his appetite for food overtook his love for music. Chubby to the point of being bloated, he returned to England in 1976 and assembled yet another incarnation of T. Rex, but by this time, his fans had deserted him. Trying to recapture credibility, he enlisted the Damned, one of England's first punk bands, as his opening act for a 1977 tour. Bolan fought hard to rebuild his career, but on September 16, 1977, the car he was a passenger in—driven by his second wife, singer Gloria Jones—careened into a chestnut tree, and Bolan was killed, just two weeks short of his thirtieth birthday.

CHAPTER SEVEN

THAT'S ALL FOLKS

Student demonstrations closed college campuses across the country during 1969 and 1970 as the trial of the "Chicago Seven" stretched from September until February 18, 1970. That day, Abbie Hoffman, Jerry Rubin, and five of their cohorts were found innocent of conspiring to incite riot outside the Chicago Democratic convention two years earlier. Protests against the Vietnam War raged on as John Lennon and the Plastic Ono Band sang "I Don't Wanna Be a Soldier Mama I Don't Wanna Die" and "Give Peace a Chance."

It wasn't until January 23, 1973, that Neil Young interrupted a New York concert to read a message that had been scribbled on a piece of paper and handed to him. "Peace has come," he told the crowd, who rejoiced for a ten-minute celebration of hugs and kisses before Young and the Stray Gators blasted into "Southern Man." On January 27, the last American soldier was killed before the official cease fire, and on February 11, U.S. POWs were released in Hanoi.

Protest rockers, especially those songwriters who could translate into words what was on the minds of so many young people, could take some credit for America's disillusionment with the war. The folk rockers of the day, most notably Bob Dylan and Crosby, Stills and Nash (and Young), led the pack.

Lyrics and melody take the front seat in this chapter. And every one of these artists owes a debt to Huddie "Leadbelly" Ledbetter, Woody Guthrie, Robert Johnson, Odetta, Phil Ochs, the Weavers, and all the other folk and hootenanny pioneers who paved the way.

Bob Dylan; Jackson Browne; the Band's Rick Danko.

THE BAND

You'd think a group of musicians simply calling themselves the Band, without a dynamic lead singer, revered guitar hero, or flashy stage act would have the odds stacked against them. But the Band was such a well-oiled backup troupe by the time they recorded their debut album—having served behind Bob Dylan and, before him, Ronnie Hawkins—that sharp musical prowess and a sturdy set of songs were all they needed to attract a dedicated following.

There was always a sort of organic, down-home, almost religious mysticism attached to the Band's songs, many of which would easily be welcome in any country singer's repertoire. Everything about the Band seemed homey, even though internal turmoil played a role in their breakup. On the inside jacket of their first album, they were even photographed surrounded by their relatives. Very quaint.

All five toured on and off in the early sixties with Arkansas rockabilly roughhouse Ronnie Hawkins and even backed him up on "Who Do You Love?" (1963). Levon Helm, also from Arkansas, played drums and was probably the group's best singer as they toured for a few years on their own after leaving Hawkins. (They were sometimes billed as the Canadian Squires, other times as Levon and the Hawks.) Guitarist Robbie Robertson, bassist Rick Danko, pianist Richard Manuel, and organist Garth Hudson, Canadians all, became

The Band (from left: Rick Danko, Levon Helm, Richard Manuel, Garth Hudson, and Robbie Robertson) were praised for their unique view of Americana in songs like "Up on Cripple Creek" and "The Night They Drove Old Dixie Down," featured on *The Band* (1969).

musical virtuosos and concert tour road hounds on those long jaunts across Canada.

Soon they landed in New York and played Greenwich Village clubs, where Bob Dylan eventually sought them out. Jam sessions between Dylan and Robertson led to the latter, along with Helm, landing spots in Dylan's electric backup band the evening he jacked up the volume on his Forest Hills concert of August 28, 1965. Some cheered the new electric Dylan, but most booed. The heckling didn't let up for their September 3 appearance at the Hollywood Bowl or for most of the autumn 1965 tour. The constant jeering drove Helm out of Dylan's troupe, and the Hawks, with Hudson, Manuel, and Danko back in at this point, found a replacement in Mickey Jones until Helm rejoined months later.

After Dylan's motorcycle crash in 1966, the Hawks followed the singer up to Woodstock, New York. They rented a large pink house in West Saugerties, New York, down the road from Dylan and went to work on what became *Music From Big Pink* (1968), the Band's debut, released on Capitol Records.

Stage Fright (1970) and *Rock of Ages* (1972) were strong albums, but after *Northern Lights—Southern Cross* (1975), the Band went to work on its coda. On Thanksgiving Day, 1976, after sixteen years of touring, the Band bid farewell in one of rock's most talked-about concerts and gracious swansongs, *The Last Waltz*. With special guests Hawkins, Neil Young, Eric Clapton, Joni Mitchell, and Van Morrison, and a stirring finale with Bob Dylan, the holiday shebang was preserved on film by Martin Scorsese and released two years later to great acclaim.

Robbie Robertson refused to join two ill-fated Band reunions in 1984 and 1985; he continues to record on his own. A third tour ended tragically on March 7, 1986, after Richard Manuel hanged himself in a motel room.

JACKSON BROWNE

A songwriter's songwriter, Jackson Browne had already written songs for Nico, Joe Cocker, Tom Rush, the Byrds, and Bonnie Raitt before releasing his self-titled debut in 1972. "Doctor My Eyes," his first hit, was a top-ten smash that made good use of his plaintive baritone croon, but it would take another four years and the release of *The Pretender* for Browne's metaphoric tales of lost love and fractured relationships to reach a wide audience.

Born in Heidelberg, Germany, Browne and his family moved to southern California when he was three years old. He played guitar in an early version of the Nitty Gritty Dirt Band and spent the winters of 1967 and 1968 in New York's Greenwich Village, where he backed folksinger Tim Buckley and wrote songs for Parisian model-turned-singer Nico. After the respected Tom Rush added a Browne song to his repertoire, the music community took notice. Browne's early admirers included the Eagles, and he cowrote their first hit, "Take It Easy."

Lost souls and affluent college kids alike related to the poignant and personal elegance Browne brought to albums like *For Everyman* (1973) and *Late for the Sky* (1974). Progressive FM radio caught up with him by 1976 and *The Pretender* became his first platinum venture. Browne

Jackson Browne played the role of political activist during the seventies after hitting the top ten with "Doctor My Eyes" in 1972.

seemed to spend the seventies growing more forlorn with each release, hitting bottom on *The Pretender* (his wife, Phyllis Major, committed suicide in March 1976). In 1978, he released his masterpiece, the relatively upbeat *Running on Empty*—an intimate account of life on the concert trail—and scored top-twenty hits with the title track and a reworking of Maurice Williams' 1960 hit "Stay."

When Browne wasn't lamenting lost love, he directed his sympathies to social causes. A booster of the Save the Whales campaign of the seventies, Browne became even more committed to saving the environment toward the end of the decade and threw all his energies into the anti–nuclear power movement. A series of "No Nukes" concerts at New York's Madison Square Garden yielded a three-record live set and an attendant motion picture, all spearheaded by Browne and some of rock's and folk's finest talents of the moment. (Bruce Springsteen and the E Street Band injected a much-needed dose of streetwise rock and roll into the event.)

Ironically, Browne's anti-nuclear efforts coincided with his finest work as an artist. Although he hit the charts several more times in the eighties—most notably in 1982 with "Somebody's Baby"—his post–No Nukes music has never matched the vitality of his seventies works.

THE BYRDS

The Byrds recognized a connection between Bob Dylan and John Lennon and parlayed the sonic union into the genesis of folk rock. Combining weighty, socially conscious lyrics with silken-smooth harmonies and ringing Rickenbacker guitars, the Byrds carved a niche for themselves that inspired many other bands.

The original lineup all came from folk backgrounds. Singer/guitarist Gene Clark, bassist David Crosby, and twelve-string guitarist Jim McGuinn (he changed his first name to Roger in 1967) began as the Jet Set, but issued their first single, "Please Let Me Love You," backed with "It Won't Be Wrong," under the name the Beefeaters in honor of the bottle of gin that their producer, Jim Dickson, was nursing at the time. The single went nowhere.

Crosby moved to rhythm guitar, and bassist Chris Hillman and drummer Michael Clarke were added to the fold to fatten up the sound of their live performances. After they changed their name to the Byrds, misspelling the word "bird" just as the Beatles had done with "beetle," Dickson persuaded them to have a go at a Bob Dylan song, "Mr. Tambourine Man." Recorded with just McGuinn, Crosby, Clark, and a crew of studio musicians (including Leon Russell), the mix of Beatlesque high harmonies with McGuinn's jingle-jangle guitar and Dylan's potent lyrics found an instant audience. "Mr. Tambourine Man," released in April 1965, went to number one within weeks.

The album *Mr. Tambourine Man* and the follow-up, *Turn! Turn! Turn!* (released only six months later), were nothing short of folk-rock masterpieces and established the Byrds as one of the hardest-working acts in show business. "Turn! Turn! Turn!" written by Pete Seeger with a lyric adapted from the Book of Ecclesiastes, became their second number one hit. But by their third album, Gene Clark was gone; fear of flying as well as tension with McGuinn led to Clark's exit.

The Byrds (from left): David Crosby, Gene Clark, Chris Hillman, and Michael Clarke.

The Byrds entered a bit of a psychedelic phase in 1966 with the release of the *Fifth Dimension* album and the song "Eight Miles High," predating freaky excursions by the Beatles and the Beach Boys by a year. Radio programmers feared that the song condoned drug use. It was subsequently banned on many stations, even though McGuinn insisted it was written about an airplane flight to London. After *Younger Than Yesterday* (1967), which included Byrds classics "So You Want to Be a Rock 'n' Roll Star" and their best Dylan cover, "My Back Pages," Crosby was out the door, too, and moved on to work on a solo album.

With the addition of Hillman's cousin, drummer Kevin Kelley, and singer/guitarist/keyboardist Gram Parsons, the Byrds entered a country-rock phase and released *Sweetheart of the Rodeo*. But Parsons refused to tour South Africa with the band due to his opposition to apartheid, and quit after only three months. In 1970, *The Ballad of Easy Rider* appeared, along with an untitled album including the gorgeous "Chestnut Mare." Personnel changes continued, but after two more albums, the Byrds clipped their wings. A Passaic, New Jersey, show on February 24, 1973, was their last concert proper.

The original lineup re-formed for one last gasp, *Byrds*, released on the Asylum label in 1973, but there was no point in continuing. (Hillman later called the disc "embarrassing.") Crosby soldiered on with Stephen Stills, Graham Nash, and Neil Young. McGuinn, Clark, and Hillman recorded together as well as separately. Michael Clarke went to work for the trifling Firefall. Gram Parsons formed the Flying Burrito Brothers with Hillman and recorded two highly regarded country albums on his own. Parsons died amid mysterious circumstances on September 19, 1973.

CROSBY, STILLS AND NASH (AND YOUNG)

By 1968, David Crosby, Stephen Stills, and Graham Nash had had their fill of rock bands. Crosby had flown from the Byrds the year before, after they had refused to record "Triad," a song about a ménage à trois that the Jefferson Airplane eventually included on *Crown of Creation*. Stills began jamming with Crosby after Buffalo Springfield threw in the towel in May. Nash had grown disillusioned with the Hollies after they refused to record his "Marrakesh Express." Their decision to release an album of Bob Dylan covers didn't sit well with Nash either.

So the three called themselves simply Crosby, Stills and Nash and released an album in 1969 bearing that name. The disc went double-platinum on the strength of the songwriting and the infectious harmonies, best exemplified on the seven-minute "Suite: Judy Blue Eyes," which Stills wrote for singer Judy Collins. By mid-1969, Stills' friend (and sometimes foe) from Buffalo Springfield, Neil Young, joined them for a summer tour.

David Crosby, Neil Young, Stephen Stills, and Graham Nash (from left, with bassist Greg Reeves): all four were accomplished singer/songwriters with impressive rock résumés before they joined forces for CSN&Y.

With Young on board, the band had an ace in the hole and released the equally strong *Deja Vu* in 1970. After four students were shot dead at Kent State University, Young penned the potent "Ohio," which was released as a single in 1970. But CSN&Y was as volatile as it was creative, and when their live album, *4 Way Street*, was released in 1971, they were already splitsville.

The other members of the group were somewhat enamored of Young. The second half of their live performances often began with each member taking a solo turn. Young usually had to go last, as his colleagues preferred not to follow him.

Without Young, the band could only be considered lightweight, and their *CSN* (1977), *Replay* (1980), and *Daylight Again* (1982) albums were not met with enthusiastic reviews. Young returned for one more swing, *American Dream* (1988), mostly as a favor to David Crosby, whose years of substance abuse had taken their toll. Young's presence revitalized the outfit, but their reunion was kept to a one-shot.

THAT'S ALL FOLKS

BOB DYLAN

Classic rock knows no greater wordsmith than Bob Dylan. Blessed with a consummate ability to spin a phrase with penetrating insight, his talent is almost supernatural.

Dylan disciples not only commit his words to memory, they live by them: his songs are covered by everyone from church choirs to cabaret crooners; fellow songwriters revere him; presidential candidates quote him.

Interestingly, Dylan didn't begin as a songwriter. Only two of the thirteen songs on his 1962 debut, *Bob Dylan*, were his own compositions. In 1962, not many singers sang their own material; Dylan changed those rules. On *The Freewheelin' Bob Dylan* (1963), all the songs were his. Dylan opened the door for vocalists to express themselves in their own words, and by the end of the decade the practice was de rigueur.

Not everyone loved Dylan. Early on, many critics couldn't get past his nasal delivery and dismissed him as a ball of hype. When he showed up in a black leather jacket at the Newport Folk Festival in 1965 and strapped on an electric guitar, folk purists booed mercilessly, cried sellout, and accused him of treason. (For years, fans have left Dylan gigs frustrated by his custom of rearranging his songs in performance, sometimes to the point of unrecognizability.) But like all mavericks, Dylan couldn't care less about what critic and concertgoers had to say.

Born Robert Allen Zimmerman on May 24, 1941, in Duluth, Minnesota, he and his family moved north to Hibbing when he was six years old. In high school he played piano, learned guitar chords, and jammed in several rock bands. By late 1959, he was enrolled at the University of Minnesota and spent most of his time in local

Bob Dylan, in the woods of Woodstock, New York; he is undoubtedly one of the most influential figures in the history of rock.

coffeehouses singing folk songs by Leadbelly, Big Bill Broonzy, and his unassailable hero, Woody Guthrie.

Rock legend has it that young Zimmerman took poet Dylan Thomas' first name as his own last name and became Bob Dylan, although he has refuted this story. He has told more than one interviewer that he took the name from his uncle Dillon and merely changed the spelling.

By January 1961, Dylan was in New York with two missions: the first was to track down Guthrie; the second was to become a singer. He found Guthrie at New Jersey's Greystone Hospital and made regular trips to win the sage's blessing. And soon Dylan was playing regularly at Village clubs such as the Commons, the Gas Light, and Gerde's Folk City, where he was spotted one evening by *New York Times* folk critic Robert Shelton. Shelton was knocked out by Dylan's performance and wrote a laudatory review, and Dylan was signed to Columbia Records by talent scout John Hammond the day after publication.

Dylan's first album was recorded in a matter of hours, was released before his twenty-first birthday, and sold a paltry five thousand copies. But Columbia Records gave their protégé time to grow, and by the time his fourth album, *Another Side of*

Dylan didn't play the legendary Woodstock concert, but did perform an hour-long set at England's Isle of Wight Pop Festival (above) that same month, August 1969.

Bob Dylan (1964), was released, Dylan was playing to packed houses. With just his acoustic guitar and harmonica in tow, he played more than two hundred shows in 1964 and knocked audiences out with "Blowin' in the Wind" (his most covered song), "The Times They Are a-Changin'," "Chimes of Freedom," "My Back Pages," and many others. His second single, "Like a Rolling Stone" (1965), shot to number two and broke the three-minute barrier for singles.

A motorcycle crash in July 1966 sidelined Dylan temporarily, but in 1968 he returned to the public arena with the *John Wesley Harding* album. More strong albums of songs about "objection, obsession, and rejection" followed, most notably *The Basement Tapes* in 1975 (the legitimate release of the oft-bootlegged sessions from his stay in Woodstock in 1966), the wrenching *Blood on the Tracks* in 1975 (the favorite of many Dylan fans, including his son, Jesse), *Desire* (1975), *Street Legal* (1978), *Shot of Love* (1981), and *Infidels* (1983). Dylan has released his writings and lyrics in book form, has appeared in films, and continues to play to sold-out houses well into his fifties.

His biggest honor came on October 16, 1992, when an eclectic group of musicians including George Harrison, Tom Petty, Eric Clapton, Johnny Cash, Pearl Jam's Eddie Vedder and Mike McCready, Stevie Wonder, and Neil Young performed his compositions at New York's Madison Square Garden. Young affectionately dubbed it a "Bobfest."

JONI MITCHELL

As the seventies began, singers who wrote their own material were more in vogue than ever before. When it came to confessional love songs, few delivered with more panache than Joni Mitchell. It may be difficult to assess just where Mitchell's acoustic, jazz-tinged soliloquies fit in the evolution of classic rock, but her music was an integral part of the genre.

Born on November 7, 1943, in Alberta, Canada, Roberta Joan Anderson learned to play guitar and ukelele, and sang Kingston Trio songs at any sing-along that would have her. She married and performed with folksinger Chuck Mitchell after moving to Toronto, but the marriage didn't last. By 1967, she was in New York and quickly gaining attention as a songwriter. Judy Collins recorded Mitchell's "Both Sides Now" and took it into the top ten. Tom Rush and Fairport Convention recorded Mitchell songs, too.

The public didn't hear Joni's gentle voice until David Crosby produced her debut album in 1968. *Joni Mitchell* and her second release, *Clouds* (1969), didn't set any sales records, but did pave the way for what followed: four strong albums in a row—*Ladies of the Canyon* (1970), *Blue* (1971), *For the Roses* (1972), and *Court and Spark* (1974).

An intimate recording full of open-tuned chords and minor keys, *Blue* established Mitchell as one of folk rock's finest artists. *Court and Spark* broadened her audience even more, with her highest-charting single, "Help Me." But from there, Mitchell dived deeper into more experimental, jazzier material. She hardly gained new fans as critics accused her of creative fatigue and questioned her intentions on her mid-seventies albums, *The Hissing of Summer Lawns*, *Hejira*, and *Don Juan's Reckless Daughter*. A collaboration with jazz bassist Charles Mingus, titled *Mingus*, followed. She was still recording in the eighties and into the nineties, though at nowhere near the pace of her halcyon years.

From 1968 to 1980, hardly a year went by without a new album release from Canadian Joni Mitchell, a songwriter's songwriter.

SIMON AND GARFUNKEL

Paul Simon and Art Garfunkel, both from Queens, New York, parlayed Simon's tender lyrics and Garfunkel's soaring tenor into a string of hit singles and best-selling albums that are considered prime vintage folk rock.

Classmates at Forest Hills High School, they dubbed themselves Tom and Jerry and landed on the charts while they were still teenagers with a single called "Hey Schoolgirl." The Simon tune, inspired by the Everly Brothers, climbed to a respectable number fifty-four on the charts and earned them two appearances on Dick Clark's television show *American Bandstand*, but it would be six years before they recorded again.

Wednesday Morning, 3 A.M., their debut, was a collection of traditional and modern folk songs, including a version of Bob Dylan's "The Times They Are a-Changin'." The somber album failed to find a sizable audience, and the duo went separate ways. Producer Tom Wilson, though, heard potential in "The Sounds of Silence," and rereleased it as a single with a new backing track, including electric guitars.

Art Garfunkel (left) and Paul Simon appealed to a cross-generational audience, who found them both perceptive and lyrical.

The record made it to number one in December 1965. So Simon and Garfunkel re-formed and launched a career that lasted for only six years but yielded the classic albums *Sounds of Silence* and *Parsley, Sage, Rosemary, and Thyme* (both in 1966), *Bookends* (1968), and *Bridge Over Troubled Water* (1970), and top-ten singles "Homeward Bound," "I Am a Rock," "The Boxer," "Cecilia," and "Mrs. Robinson," in which Simon pays respect to his boyhood idol, New York Yankee Joe DiMaggio. Years later, when Simon appeared on *The Dick Cavett Show* alongside Mickey Mantle, the Mick asked why he wasn't the subject of a Simon and Garfunkel song. Simon replied that he needed the extra syllables.

At the peak of their career together, Simon and Garfunkel decided to pursue other interests. Simon continued a prosperous solo career while Garfunkel acted in motion pictures and recorded as well. In 1975 they joined together again for one more top-ten single, the brisk "My Little Town," and played scattershot concert appearances well into the next decade. A free concert in New York's Central Park resulted in the best-selling double album *The Concert in Central Park* (1982).

JAMES TAYLOR

Few voices in rock are as instantly recognizable as the sweet-as-honey sound that James Taylor was blessed with. His warm voice has been nearly as vital an ingredient in his lengthy career as his songwriting. His style, so often imitated, is based on the simple combination of voice and acoustic guitar. He's considered the archetypal singer/songwriter, yet some of his biggest hits were written by others. Carole King's "You've Got a Friend" in 1971 was his first to hit number one. A revamped "Mockingbird" was a top-five hit in 1974 for Taylor and his then-wife, Carly Simon.

Born March 12, 1948, in Boston and reared there and in Chapel Hill, North Carolina, Taylor was a troubled teenager who didn't care for the Massachusetts boarding school his parents sent him to. He sank into deep depression and was put under observation at a psychiatric hospital for several months before venturing to New York in 1967. He took up with a four-piece band called the Flying Machine and played the Greenwich Village circuit, but was soon back in Chapel Hill, trying to shake an addiction to heroin.

Attempting to change his luck in England, Taylor eventually became one of the first artists to sign a record deal with Apple, the Beatles' label, and

James Taylor's confessionals paired folk-influenced guitar music with deeply emotional lyrics.

released his self-titled debut album in 1969. The record did little to advance his career, even with the tender ballad "Carolina on My Mind," and Taylor retreated deeper into drugs. He returned to the States and checked into yet another mental institution, this time for a five-month stay.

In 1970, Taylor signed with Warner Bros. records and went to work on his second release, *Sweet Baby James*, which brought him his first hit single, "Fire and Rain," written over a three-month period in 1968, some of it during his stay at the institution. His next release, *Mud Slide Slim and the Blue Horizon* (1971), included his reading of "You've Got a Friend," and his career took off. All his albums through the seventies sold comparatively well, most notably *Gorilla* (1975) and *JT* (1977), even as critics began to accuse him of effusive sentimentality.

Something of an activist, Taylor campaigned for Jimmy Carter in 1976 and for John Anderson in 1980, and was a major player in the No Nukes movement and other causes. His marriage to Simon ended in 1982, one year after the single "Her Town Too."

SOUTHERN SWING AND BARROOM BOOGIE

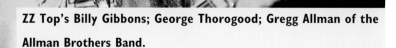

ZZ Top's Billy Gibbons; George Thorogood; Gregg Allman of the Allman Brothers Band.

They were so proud of their roots. The southern rockers sang about their home and heritage with more passion than those in any other rock movement. Dickey Betts wrote "Southbound" for the Allman Brothers Band in 1973; Lynyrd Skynyrd sang "Sweet Home Alabama" in 1974; Charlie Daniels predicted "The South's Gonna Do It" in 1975. Was it merely a coincidence that Jimmy Carter, the then-governor of Georgia, began his successful presidential campaign the same year as Daniels' hit? Carter, turned on by his son Chip to the Allman Brothers Band and Bob Dylan, was the first presidential candidate to embrace rock and roll. He even invited Dylan to the governor's mansion in January of 1974. "He never initiates conversation," Carter told *Rolling Stone* about Dylan. "But he'll answer a question if you ask him."

Tragic accidents seem to strike more in southern rock than in any other subgenre. Duane Allman died in a horrible motorcycle tragedy in 1971. A year later, a bike accident claimed bassist Berry Oakley, too. In 1977, the crash of Lynyrd Skynyrd's private plane took the lives of singer Ronnie Van Zant, guitarist Steve Gaines, and others. By 1979, southern rock's glory years were fading as Capricorn Records, whose president, Phil Walden, was the movement's chief proponent, filed for bankruptcy.

It was a seventies movement that didn't last long past the end of the decade, but rock fans north of the Mason-Dixon line and the world over scarfed up butt-kickin' albums from the Allmans, Skynyrd, and the Marshall Tucker Band. Later in the seventies came George Thorogood and the Destroyers, whose barroom boogie remains in steady rotation on classic rock radio.

The artists in this chapter are all a little bit country and a little bit rock and roll, and all owe a debt to country legends like Hank Williams, George Jones, Loretta Lynn, Ernest Tubb, Merle Haggard, and Johnny Cash as well as blues greats like Blind Lemon Jefferson, Charley Patton, Lightnin' Hopkins, Howlin' Wolf, and other lesser-known heroes.

THE ALLMAN BROTHERS BAND

Duane and Gregg Allman didn't get it right the first time around. Or the second, for that matter. As teenagers in Florida, they formed the Allman Joys and recorded a single, a version of Willie Dixon's "Spoonful," which failed to spark interest. So they moved to Los Angeles, formed the Hourglass, and signed with Liberty Records. But after two albums of cover material failed to catch on, they were back in Florida.

In the hands of Duane Allman, a guitar sang like a bird. Even before the Allman Brothers hit, he was a studio session guitarist very much in demand and played on Wilson Pickett's version of "Hey Jude," as well as on sessions with rhythm and blues heavyweights Percy Sledge, Clarence Carter, and Aretha Franklin. (That's Duane playing slide on 'Retha's version of the Band's "The Weight.") On the strength of his six-string skill, Duane landed a deal with Capricorn Records and quickly set his mind to assembling a band.

Duane and Gregg had played with drummer Butch Trucks in a group called the 31st of February, so Trucks was in. Jai Johanny Johanson, a Muscle Shoals studio hound, was recruited as second trapsman. From the band

It was the guitar interplay among Dickey Betts (above) and the brothers Allman that put the Allman Brothers Band a step ahead of the southern rock pack.

Second Coming came guitarist Dickey Betts and bassist Berry Oakley.

Their 1969 debut album, *The Allman Brothers Band*, was a hit with rock critics, who predicted the dawning of a southern rock movement based on the Allman Brothers' blend of blues, country, swing, bluegrass, and plenty of boogie supplied by Duane and Dickey's guitar licks and Gregg's organ fills. By the time their third record—*At Fillmore East* (1971), one of rock's most satisfying live records—was released, the Allman Brothers Band were one of rock's biggest attractions. Audiences howled at their revved-up takes on blues standards like "Stormy Monday" and "Statesboro Blues," as well as original compositions like Gregg's "Whipping Post," which ran over twenty minutes in concert and took up the entire fourth side of the live album.

Duane Allman continued his extracurricular studio work with notables Boz Scaggs, Ronnie Hawkins, and Laura Nyro, and was a key figure with Eric Clapton in Derek and the Dominoes, but tragedy struck on October 29, 1971, when Allman was killed in a motorcycle accident in Macon, Georgia. He was only twenty-four.

Duane had already recorded three tracks for the Allmans' next record, *Eat a Peach*, and more of his work was added when additional live tape from the Fillmore shows turned *Eat a Peach* into a double

album. But tragedy struck again on November 11, 1972, this time to Oakley, who was killed in a motorcycle crash just three blocks from where Duane's accident had occurred the year before. Lamar Williams replaced Oakley.

Brothers and Sisters came next and went all the way to number one, on the strength of "Ramblin' Man," the Allman Brothers' first hit single (written by Betts, by then the unofficial leader of the group). Dissension struck after that, mostly between Gregg Allman and Betts, and album releases through the seventies were infrequent and were recorded around solo excursions. In 1976,

An alternate shot from this photo session graced the cover of At *Fillmore East*. From left: Jai Johanny Johanson, Duane Allman, Gregg Allman, Berry Oakley, Dickey Betts, and Butch Trucks (with hat).

Allman testified in a drug trial against his road manager, Scooter Herring, and Herring was sentenced to seventy-five years in the slammer. Allman's testimony infuriated the others, who vowed never to play with him again.

After further solo ventures, the Allman Brothers Band buried the hatchet, re-formed in 1978, and hit the singles chart twice more with "Crazy Love" and "Straight From the Heart," only to break up again in the early eighties, then re-form yet again in 1989 for a road tour. Since then, they have staged various concert treks, always to enthusiastic response.

THE CHARLIE DANIELS BAND

With a tip of his Stetson to the Allman Brothers Band, session guitarist and seasoned fiddler Charlie Daniels formed his own band in 1971—with twin lead guitarists and two drummers, just like his counterparts—and lassoed a string of seventies hits for himself, most notably "Uneasy Rider," "The South's Gonna Do It," and his signature hit from 1979, "The Devil Went Down to Georgia." A good-humored, burly rabble-rouser out of Wilmington, North Carolina, with a smile for everyone he met, Daniels heart was as big as his belly.

His first band was the Jaguars, who blew the roof off many a honky-tonk and roadhouse south of the Mason-Dixon line from 1958 to 1967. In 1968, he moved to Nashville and became a session musician, lending his talents to a diverse crop of artists, such as Ringo Starr, Leonard Cohen,

North Carolina's Charlie Daniels (right) was a seasoned session guitarist and fiddler who was very much in demand before forming his own band in 1971.

and Pete Seeger, and a number of country singers as well. He played on Bob Dylan's country ode *Nashville Skyline* in 1969 and produced four records for the Youngbloods.

With his own band, Charlie became a country-rock star and played to turn-away audiences with boogie-juiced albums like *Fire on the Mountain* (1974) and *Saddle Tramp* (1976), but his first hit, "Uneasy Rider," was more of a novelty number. In 1974, he initiated the annual Volunteer Jam concerts in Nashville, and in 1979, at the height of the disco era, Daniels rode "The Devil Went Down to Georgia" all the way to number three on the singles chart. CDB continued to record through the eighties and into the nineties, scoring an occasional country hit now and then, and playing every country-rock bill that would have them.

LITTLE FEAT

They might have come from southern California, but Little Feat sounded more southern than California. Although they never broke any sales records—only their 1979 live album, *Waiting for Columbus*, went gold—Little Feat were mighty influential and amassed a dedicated cult following in the ten years they played together.

Lowell George, with his warm, bluesy vocals and graceful slide guitar, was Little Feat's linchpin, but not many rock fans are aware of George's colorful pre-Feat biography. As a kid, he and his brother appeared on *Ted Mack's Original Amateur Hour*. George played flute in the Hollywood High School Orchestra; contributed oboe and baritone sax to recording sessions for Frank Sinatra; joined cult bands called the Seeds and the Standells for brief runs; and formed a folk-rock group called the Factory in the mid-sixties. When the Factory split up, George played guitar in Frank Zappa's Mothers of Invention, contributing to classic Zappa albums *Weasels Ripped My Flesh* and, although he's not credited, *Hot Rats*.

With George, drummer Richie Hayward from the Mothers, pianist Bill Payne, and bassist Roy Estrada, Little Feat took their first steps in

Even before his Little Feat days, Lowell George had been recognized as a songwriting talent: two of his early compositions, "Willin'" and "Truck Stop Girl," were performed by the Byrds.

1969, and their self-titled debut album was in the stores soon after. (Supposedly, their name comes from a sarcastic remark made about George's feet by Mothers drummer Jimmy Carl Black.) The album sold poorly, as did their second release, *Sailin' Shoes*. Estrada left and was replaced by Kenny Gradney, and Little Feat expanded into an eclectic funk-rock six-piece band.

Dixie Chicken (1973), probably their best album, was next. And although that album didn't sell in huge numbers either, Warner Bros. Records never let the band go, and Little Feat recorded five more albums, two of them live, before George formed his own band in 1978 and announced Little Feat's breakup.

George produced *Shakedown Street* for the Grateful Dead at about this time, released a solo album, *Thanks I'll Eat It Here*, and toured with his own band. But his weight ballooned and his health took a dive. On June 29, 1979, Lowell George died at age thirty-four from a heart attack related to drug problems and obesity. He was in Arlington, Virginia, at the time, and had played his final gig just the night before at George Washington University.

LYNYRD SKYNYRD

"What song is it you wanna hear?"

That question, posed on Lynyrd Skynyrd's 1976 live album, *One More for the Road*, is forever etched in the memories of rock fans, as is the answer: "'Free Bird' !!!" So renowned is this exchange between performer and audience that as long as there are rock concerts, there will always be a wisenheimer in the cheap seats requesting "Free Bird" no matter who is on stage.

Leonard Skinner was the name of a physical education teacher in Jacksonville, Florida, who had a thing against guys with long hair. It's a good guess he made Ronnie Van Zant, Gary Rossington, and Allen Collins run extra laps during gym. So captivated with Skinner were the three pupils that they changed the name of their rock trio from My Backyard to a joke version of Skinner's name. Where's ol' Len today?

In 1973, Lynyrd Skynyrd's lineup was intact with three guitarists on board (Rossington, Collins, and Ed King from Strawberry Alarm Clock) and Van Zant on vocals. Unlike the Allmans, Skynyrd favored rock over the blues, although blues, country, and soul figured into their approach. Their debut album, *pronounced leh-nerd skin-nerd*, drew notice for "Free Bird," which was written in memory of Duane Allman and soon became Skynyrd's anthem. The song was released twice as a single. The studio version rose to number nineteen in 1975. Two years later, a live version made it to number thirty-eight.

Lynyrd Skynyrd earned a reputation as a great live band, and played a series of sellout tours in the mid-seventies.

After a 1973 tour with the Who, Skynyrd's second album, *Second Helping*, went gold. Included on the disc was their sole top-ten single, "Sweet Home Alabama," a retaliation directed to Neil Young for his "Southern Man" and "Alabama." But there didn't seem to be any bad blood between the two camps. Van Zant wore a Neil Young T-shirt on occasion, and Young even offered a few songs to the band, though they were never released.

After two more studio ventures, a live album appeared, recorded at Atlanta's Fox Theatre with new guitarist Steven Gaines. Now Lynyrd Skynyrd was one of America's top concert draws. But on October 20, 1977, as they embarked on another tour, Van Zant, Gaines and his sister (singer Cassie Gaines), and manager Dean Kirkpatrick were killed in an airplane crash just outside Gillsburg, Mississippi, as they were en route to Baton Rouge, Louisiana.

Skynyrd's sixth album, *Street Survivors*, had been released just three days earlier, with a cover depicting the band eerily surrounded by flames. The cover was quickly altered, and the album became one of Skynyrd's biggest sellers. The group decided not to continue, but the Rossington-Collins Band emerged, and Neil Young sang "Sweet Home Alabama" in a moving tribute in his concerts.

THE MARSHALL TUCKER BAND

The Marshall Tucker Band, favorite sons of Spartanburg, South Carolina, injected a catchy dose of swing and, later on, elements of soft jazz into their brand of southern rock. But when these hell-raisers wanted to pull out all the stops, they could. Marshall Tucker rocked out with the best of the lot.

All the members were born and raised in Spartanburg. Guitarist/singer Toy Caldwell and his younger brother, Tommy, a bassist, had rock in their blood even as teenagers. Toy played in the Rants, Tommy in the New Generation. After they were both discharged from the army in 1970, Toy formed his own band, Toy Factory, with singer Doug Gray and woodwind player Jerry Eubanks. In 1971, Tommy came aboard with guitarist George McCorkle and drummer Paul Riddle, and the new ensemble christened themselves the Marshall Tucker Band in honor of a piano tuner who owned one of the rehearsal halls they practiced in.

The members of fellow southern band Wet Willie caught a Marshall Tucker set and suggested that they get in touch with Phil Walden at Capricorn Records about a deal. They did, and the Marshall Tucker Band enjoyed a six-album career that lasted through the seventies, highlighted by their first hit single, "Can't You See?" along with "Fire on the Mountain," "This Ol' Cowboy," and their highest-charting single, "Heard It in a Love Song."

Tommy Caldwell died on April 28, 1980, six days after an automobile accident in Spartanburg. Franklin Wilkie replaced him, and the band continued to release albums well into the eighties, but after Caldwell's death, the Marshall Tucker Band's glory years were behind them.

THE OUTLAWS

Florida's Outlaws, like most southern rockers, took their cue from the Allmans, but boasted three guitarists at the outset: Hughie Thomasson, Billy Jones, and Henry Paul; Monty Yoho and Frank O'Keefe (replaced by Harvey Arnold in 1977) joined them on drums and bass, respectively. Unlike Gregg and Duane's crew, the Outlaws favored strong Eagleslike vocal harmonies.

Written off by critics as lightweights—"Outlaws my ass" read the record review in New York's *Village Voice*—the Outlaws did attract a hefty fan

The Outlaws, led by Hughie Thomasson (center), hold the distinction of being the first band signed to the Arista label.

base through the seventies, beginning in 1974 with their debut and continuing well into the eighties. Chart-toppers they weren't. "There Goes Another Love Song" and "(Ghost) Riders in the Sky" were their only top-forty singles, but when they stretched "Green Grass and High Tides" into an extended jam, they were lethal. Their fans are so faithful that the Outlaws are more than just the answer to the trivia question "What was the first group that record executive Clive Davis signed to his Arista label?"

GEORGE THOROGOOD AND THE DESTROYERS

There's a good reason for including the term "barroom boogie" in this chapter: George Thorogood had to be included somewhere. With their butt-kickin', straight-ahead brand of guitar-blazing blues-rock, Thorogood's Destroyers are the perfect bar and party band.

George wasn't from the South. He was born in Wilmington, Delaware, and assembled his Destroyers—bassist Billy Blough and drummer Jeff Simon—in 1973. He scored a record deal with the independent Rounder label and released his debut in 1977, followed by *Move It on Over* (1978). It was the dawning of the punk era, but George's slide-guitar raunch 'n' roll—inspired by blues and rock legends like John Lee Hooker, Bo Diddley, Muddy Waters, Elmore James, and Chuck Berry—found an instant audience with rock fans eager to pick up the beat, but still a bit fearful of the punks.

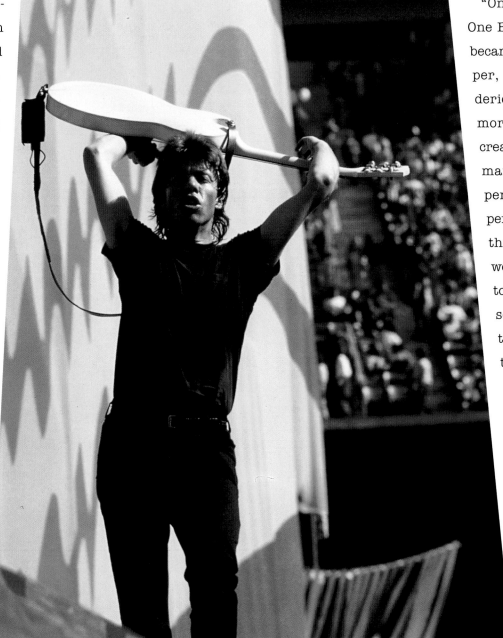

George Thorogood and the Destroyers came from Delaware, but their brand of rock has always been rooted in southern boogie.

"One Bourbon, One Scotch, One Beer," written by Hooker, became Thorogood's showstopper, but he's always been derided by rock purists as more of a carbon-copy re-creator than a genuine blues-man with his own distinct personality. Ergo, he's the perfect opening act. He'll get the crowd pumped up but won't step on the headliner's toes. The Rolling Stones sensed this and tapped him to open several dates on their 1981 tour.

George played semi-pro baseball in 1980, but was back with the Destroyers by 1981, once playing fifty states in fifty days. He has spent his time since then rockin' bars and honky-tonks the world over. His lightning boogie-rock is timeless. As long as he has hands, he'll be working that slide.

ZZ TOP

They always come last in any alphabetical survey of musical groups, but ZZ Top was the first classic rock band to parlay Texas boogie into a hugely successful career. Not only could they cook, they had the best beards in rock and roll. (Ironically, the guy in the band named Beard rarely sported one.)

Billy Gibbons played guitar in a psychedelic band out of Houston called Moving Sidewalks. Their local hit single, "99th Floor," earned them an opening slot on a 1968 tour with Jimi Hendrix, but their 1969 album, *Flash*, could have been called Flash in the Pan. The group went splitsville the next year, after some of the members were called to the Vietnam War.

Gibbons and his manager, Bill Ham, eventually recruited bassist Dusty Hill and drummer Frank Beard from a Dallas band called American Blues and, with the absurd name ZZ Top, released their debut, the aptly titled *ZZ Top's First Album*,

ZZ Top's Dusty Hill (left) and Billy Gibbons are renowned for their extravagant beards. The drummer, named Frank Beard, rarely wore the trademark fall of facial hair.

in 1970. They toured the South extensively and in 1973 scored their first hit, "La Grange," a song about the bordello later immortalized in the Broadway musical *The Best Little Whorehouse in Texas*.

The year 1975 brought ZZ Top's first top-forty single, "Tush," as their following doubled. In 1976, they brought a bit of Texas to their concert set and adorned the stage with snakes, cacti, cattle, and real live buffalo. One concert audience supposedly had the daylights scared out of them when some of the wildlife ventured into the seats.

ZZ Top went on a two-year hiatus in 1977, but returned in high style with the fiery *Deguello* album in 1979, maybe their best. The MTV era of the eighties ushered in another phase for ZZ Top as "Gimme All Your Lovin'," "Legs," "Sharp-Dressed Man," "Sleeping Bag," and "Rough Boy" became radio favorites and endlessly repeated videos (with the requisite comely models) on the popular music-video channel.

Peter Frampton; Heart's Nancy Wilson; Meat Loaf and friend.

RADIO-READY ROCKERS

Rockers of the sixties set out to tear down walls that were finally collapsing by the mid-seventies. Presidential candidate Jimmy Carter's admiration for Bob Dylan and the Allman Brothers earned rock a bit of respect from older generations, even as gay-lib, women's-lib, and what's-your-lib movements picked up more steam. In June 1974, America's Little League allowed girls to play baseball for the first time, and in September of that year, draft evaders of the Vietnam War were pardoned provided they perform community service. In October 1975, a television program called *Saturday Night Live* premiered and re-energized live music and comedy on television. An appearance on the popular program could not only sell records, it could launch careers.

In January 1977, Carter took office, and in June of that year, New York followed other states in decriminalizing small amounts of marijuana. (Six years had passed since Brewer & Shipley sang "One Toke Over the Line.")

Disco was gaining popularity, and the punk movement, launched in New York and London, was introducing a new breed of rebellious rockers led by the Ramones and the Sex Pistols. What was the punk's beef? Big fat, corporate rock. Rock was a huge industry by the seventies and the big bands of the day—many composed of hangers-on from the sixties, others fresh faces with dollar signs in their eyes—scrambled for radio airplay, major concert tours, and a shot at the big time and the high life.

BAD COMPANY

It's no surprise that Bad Company's 1974 self-titled debut album climbed straight to the top spot on *Billboard*'s album chart. Rock fans were already well acquainted with lead howler Paul Rodgers from his days with Free, and guitarist Mick Ralphs had been an integral part of Mott the Hoople. With bassist Boz Burrell from King Crimson and drummer Simon Kirke—Rodgers' pal from Free—Bad Company, at least the first incarnation, were hard-rock radio favorites in the mid-seventies with their first single, "Can't Get Enough," as well as "Bad Company," "Feel Like Makin' Love," "Shooting Star," and many others.

Ralphs struck up a friendship with Rodgers on a Free/Mott the Hoople tour and eventually realized that Rodgers' husky, little-bit-o'-soul vocals were more suitable than Hunter's for the songs Ralphs was writing at the time. So Ralphs tendered his resignation with Mott and took up with the new quartet. Taking their name from the 1972 western that starred Jeff Bridges, Bad Company played their first concert at Newcastle City Hall on March 8, 1974, and became critics' darlings right off the bat.

Their debut album was recorded in a whirlwind ten days in Ronnie Lane's mobile studio and released on their manager's (Peter Grant) label, Swan Song, home of Led Zep. One album appeared every year that followed except 1978. In 1979, they veered in another direction and added synthesizers and strings to the mix. Releases continued into the eighties, each one more mediocre than

Boz Burrell (left) had played with King Crimson, Paul Rodgers (center) and drummer Simon Kirke had been in Free, and Mick Ralphs had been with Mott the Hoople before the four united in Bad Company.

the last until the group dissolved in 1983. By 1985, Rodgers was busy singing in Jimmy Page's short-lived outfit, the Firm. A 1986 reunion album, *Fame and Fortune*, featured Brian Howe, formerly singer with Ted Nugent, as Rodgers' replacement.

BOSTON

They came out of nowhere in 1976 and ended up selling, by the mid-nineties, over eleven million copies of their debut album. There was one more release two years later, which was not as sparkling, then an eight-year break before their third. So goes the story of Boston.

Guitar wonderboy Tom Scholz from Toledo, Ohio, held a degree in mechanical engineering from MIT and worked as a senior product designer for Polaroid. In his basement studio, he toiled endlessly on the demo tape for what would become Boston's first record. Scholz's brand of rock wasn't at all innovative: just standard power-chord rock boosted by high harmonies and double-guitar leads.

After being rejected by label after label, he finally landed a deal with Epic, and a band of musicians, all from Boston, were assembled

Boston's debut album, an instant chart-topper, allowed the band to bypass the club circuit in favor of arena concerts.

behind Scholz. The debut sold half a million copies in its first two months in the stores, and Boston went straight to the head of the class, the arena circuit, where they pleased the masses with anthems like "More Than a Feeling," "Peace of Mind," and "Foreplay/Long Time."

The follow-up, *Don't Look Back* (1978), didn't raise the stakes on the debut, and concert audiences began to wane. The band took a breather and Scholz returned to the laboratory, where he patented the Rockman, a Walkman-size, headphone-equipped amplifier for practicing guitarists. The third Boston album, *Third Stage*, didn't see the light of day until 1986. By then, the old Boston fans had moved on to new interests, but their hit single "Amanda" went to number one.

FOREIGNER

In the late seventies and well into the eighties, you couldn't turn on a car radio without hearing a Foreigner song. These six guys were a classic rock hit machine. Their top-ten singles included "Feels Like the First Time," "Cold as Ice," "Hot Blooded," "Double Vision," and "Urgent." Their albums sold in megaplatinum numbers, even as critics accused Foreigner's cock-rock of being duller than dull.

Lou Gramm was the high-pitched, wailing singer who wouldn't have been out of place in an eighties heavy metal band, but Foreigner relied on multi-instrumentalist Ian McDonald and Al Greenwood's keyboards, typically verboten in metal, for their million-dollar sound.

The hits were written by guitarist Mick Jones (not to be confused with the Clash's singer/guitarist), who had been around the music-industry block before assembling Foreigner in New York in 1976. He racked up a string of British hits in the sixties with Nero and the Gladiators. He worked with Spooky Tooth, tried his hand as a record company A&R executive, then joined the Leslie West Band for a spell before teaming with McDonald. They initially planned on calling their outfit Trigger, but another band had already laid claim to that name, so Foreigner was chosen because Jones, McDonald, and drummer Dennis Elliott were British while Gramm, Greenwood, and bassist Ed Gagliardi were New Yorkers.

All of Foreigner's albums have been huge sellers, the biggest being *4* (1981). They reached their zenith in 1984, when they were joined by singer Jennifer Holliday and the New Jersey Mass Choir for Foreigner's sole number one hit, "I Want to Know What Love Is."

Guitarist Mick Jones (left, with singer Lou Gramm) had played with Spooky Tooth and the Leslie West Band before putting Foreigner together in 1976.

PETER FRAMPTON

Peter Frampton's story is the classic "here today, gone tomorrow." Frampton had the world at his feet in 1975, when the boyishly handsome guitarist with the golden locks was making a bid for superstardom. His 1976 live album, *Frampton Comes Alive!*, spent ten weeks at number one (to date, it's sold six million copies in America) and yielded three hit singles, two of those top-ten. But these days, Frampton has a tough time selling out a theater, much less an arena.

He was born in Beckenham, England, on April 22, 1950. He played in his first band, the Little Ravens, while he was still enrolled at Bromley Technical School where his father was a teacher. David Bowie was a schoolmate, but the two never performed together. Frampton's next band, a rhythm and blues outfit called the Preachers, led to a stint with the Herd, a teeny-bop band, which led to his association with ex–Small Faces singer Steve Marriott and the band Humble Pie. Frampton played guitar with the Pie through five albums,

Peter Frampton became the classic "here today, gone tomorrow" rocker. *Frampton Comes Alive!* sold six million copies in the late seventies. Today, he walks down Broadway unnoticed.

from 1968 through 1971. After the release of *Performance—Rockin' the Fillmore*, one of rock's finest live albums, he went on to his own career.

In concert, Frampton's audience grew steadily, but his first three albums conveyed none of the fire of his live shows. His fourth release, *Frampton*, was an improved effort, and in 1976, his career hit full-throttle with the release of *Frampton Comes Alive!* (recorded at San Francisco's Winterland Ballroom). His straight-ahead guitar rock, boosted by his talk-box guitar solos, found an enormous audience with songs like "Show Me the Way," "Baby I Love Your Way," and the crowd pleaser "Do You Feel Like We Do." Frampton, it seemed, could do no wrong.

But the much anticipated follow-up, *I'm in You*, only ran on the steam that *Comes Alive!* left in its wake. The movie he appeared in, *Sgt. Pepper's Lonely Hearts Club Band*, was a laughable disaster. He was injured severely in a car crash in June 1978, and later that year his girlfriend left him.

By the time his next album, *Where I Should Be*, was released, Frampton's career was in jeopardy; he has never been able to rebound. All his mid-eighties A&M releases are out of print. His albums of the nineties, released on a small, independent label, have all stalled at the gate.

THE J. GEILS BAND

Peter Blankenfield called himself Woofuh Goofuh on his WBCN radio show out of Boston. In his band called the Hallucinations he was rhythm and blues belter Peter Wolf. In 1967, after the Hallucinations evaporated, Wolf and the band's drummer, Stephen Jo Bladd, drifted to bassist Danny Klein, harmonica player "Magic" Dick Salwitz, and guitarist J. (Jerome) Geils of the J. Geils Blues Band. They dropped the Blues from the name and took to perfecting their stage act as greasers, with black leather jackets, slicked-back hair, and a repertoire of rock tunes owing much to rhythm and blues and doo-wop. (Wolf is an avid doo-wop collector.)

The J. Geils Band released ten top-forty hits between 1972 and 1982, hitting a high point in 1981–1982 with "Centerfold" and "Freeze Frame," while touring constantly. A name change to Geils in 1977 didn't last long. In 1983, Wolf split for a solo career, and the remaining members recorded one last album, the forgettable *You're Getting Even While I'm Gettin' Old*, before calling it a day.

Peter Wolf (right) was the singer, lyricist, and front man for the band who named itself after Jerome Geils.

THE GUESS WHO

The songs "American Woman," "No Time," and "No Sugar Tonight" and the amusing story of how they got their name have earned the Guess Who a place in classic rock history.

In Winnipeg, Manitoba, in the mid-sixties, they were known as Chad Allan and the Expressions (a name that had evolved from Allan and the Silvertones, then the Reflections). After cutting a version of "Shakin' All Over," an early-sixties British hit, the Expressions' record company, Scepter, thought the name was too long and "old-sounding." So they turned the problem into a contest and credited the song to "Guess Who?"

Problem was, radio DJs started calling the band the Guess Who. When "Shakin' All Over" went to number one, they had passed the point of no return. Scepter thought it would be suicide to change the name again, so the Guess Who they became.

In 1965, Allan left and was replaced by Burton Cummings, who, along with guitarist Randy Bachman, led the Guess Who through its own Canadian television show, *Where It's At*, and several Canadian singles before breaking through in America with a string of hits that began in 1969 with "These Eyes."

In 1970, Bachman became a Mormon and announced his decision to leave, due in part to tension with Cummings and the band's wild lifestyle. Bachman eventually formed the Bachman-Turner Overdrive with his brothers Tim and Robbie, and enjoyed renewed success with a batch of successful singles.

HEART

Is there a place for women in hard rock? Ask the Wilson sisters from Seattle, who have sold millions of records with Heart and have probably opened more doors for women in the boys' club of rock than any other band. Critics may suggest that Heart is nothing more than Led Zep cock-rock done up with comely female vocals. But as bombastic as Heart might be, they have successfully avoided the silly extravagance and hot-winded bluster that accompanies many female metal acts in favor of a solid repertoire of highly melodic pop-rock fare.

Ann Wilson joined the all-male band known as Heart in 1970 while her younger sister Nancy performed as a folksinger in their native Seattle. Nancy had cased her acoustic guitar in 1974 for a career with Heart, just as the band was forced to move north to Vancouver to avoid the military draft, which had its eye on Roger Fisher, Heart's guitarist and Ann's boyfriend.

Steady gigging around British Columbia won the band a record deal with Canada's Mushroom label. Their debut album, *Dreamboat Annie*, was an instant hit in Canada as well as in the U.S., where the disc eventually sold more than two million copies on the strength of heavy radio airplay and two catchy singles, "Crazy on You" and "Magic Man."

So when Heart returned to America as bankable rock stars, they signed a new record deal with Portrait, a CBS subsidiary, even though the band was still under contract to Mushroom. Prolonged legal battles ensued, until a judge ultimately decided that Heart could go to Portrait, and Mushroom could release the band's second album, *Magazine*, but only if the sisters had a chance to remix what they felt

Heart's Ann (left) and Nancy Wilson, sisters from Seattle, have made inroads for women in rock with their solid collection of pop-rock hits.

was a mediocre record. (*Magazine* became Heart's third release. *Little Queen*, the band's first for Portrait, became their second album.)

By their fifth album, *Bebe le Strange*, Heart was one of rock's biggest acts and scored a top-ten hit with a reworking of Aaron Neville's 1967 single, "Tell It Like It Is." Through the eighties, Heart kept revisiting the singles chart—"These Dreams" hit number one in 1986; "Alone" did the same a year later—while their albums continued to sell steadily.

MEAT LOAF

"Paradise by the Dashboard Light," a mini rock-opera about two young backseat lovers eager to take the plunge, was all Meat Loaf needed to turn himself into a household name and turn his 1977 album, *Bat Out of Hell*, into a multimillion blockbuster. No other rock song has ever made better use of the talents of baseball Hall of Famer, New York Yankees shortstop and sportscaster, Phil "Scooter" Rizzuto. To date, *Bat Out of Hell* has sold more than nine million copies in America. Holy cash cow!

Marvin Lee Aday was born in Dallas on September 27, 1948, and was blessed with the nickname Meat Loaf by his high school football coach. He toured in a national company of *Hair* before meeting a singer named Stoney and recording *Featuring Stoney and Meat Loaf* for the Rare Earth label in 1971. The record went nowhere, but the Loaf stuck to his guns. He played the role of Eddie in the highly regarded cult film *The Rocky Horror Picture Show* and sang lead vocals on Ted Nugent's *Free for All* album. Along the way he met Jim Steinman, a songwriter with a demo tape of strong songs, and rehearsed for a full year with Steinman before securing a record

Before recording the blockbuster *Bat Out of Hell*, Meat Loaf appeared off-Broadway and in the cult film *The Rocky Horror Picture Show*.

deal with Epic and the production wizardry of Todd Rundgren.

Meat Loaf took to the concert circuit with a seven-piece band that included singer Karla Devito, and *Bat Out of Hell* became bigger than the Loaf's waistline. "Paradise by the Dashboard Light" was acted out on stage every night and eventually became a kooky but colossal FM radio hit. Rizzuto—who recorded a phony play-by-play of the back-seat liaison for the song's bridge—insisted that he had been duped into the whole charade and called Loaf a huckleberry. (Loaf made sure that Scooter was awarded a gold record.)

The tour and the overnight success took a toll on Mr. Loaf, as the *New York Times* referred to him. He'd often pass out backstage between encores. And he learned that success was difficult to duplicate. Subsequent releases in the eighties fell flat. It wasn't until 1993, and the release of *Bat Out of Hell II: Back into Hell*, that Meat Loaf, at that point several pounds lighter, would once again sell millions of records.

STEELY DAN

They were consummate studio perfectionists who bowed out of the concert-tour circuit as early as 1974. Steely Dan's particular brand of heady jazz-tinged rock might sound middle-of-the-road by today's standards, but in the mid-seventies, the band, headed by Walter Becker and Donald Fagen, didn't sound tame at all to rock fans who stayed with the group and bought thousands of their records even as they delved deeper into tepid jazz experiments near the decade's end.

Becker, a singer-bassist, and Fagen, a singer-keyboardist, met at Bard College in 1967 and played in various rock bands, one with actor-comedian Chevy Chase, before leaving Bard—Becker was expelled, Fagen got the degree—and procuring jobs with ABC records as songwriters. (Barbra Streisand recorded their "I Mean to Shine.") Along the way, they played in the road band for Jay and the Americans, and developed an early distaste for touring before nabbing a recording deal with ABC in 1972. By December, they had their first hit: "Do It Again" went all the way to number six for Steely Dan, the name taken for a steam-powered dildo in William Burroughs' celebrated novel *Naked Lunch*.

Through the years, Steely Dan members came and went, but the project always revolved around Becker and Fagen. In 1974, they gave up touring altogether after the promotional swing for their third album, *Pretzel Logic*, and concentrated exclusively on studio work. Their lyrics were often self-indulgent and perplexing, but that didn't stop progressive radio from airing "My Old School," "Bad Sneakers," "Doctor Wu," "Black Friday," and any others, including the hit singles "Reelin' in the Years" (number eleven, 1973) and "Rikki Don't Lose That Number" (number four, 1974).

Royal Scam (1976) was a low point, but Steely Dan rebounded the following year with their biggest record, *Aja*. Easily accessible melodies in

Donald Fagen (above) and Walter Becker were the heart and soul of Steely Dan. Early in their careers, both were members of Jay and the Americans.

"Peg," "Deacon Blues," and "Josie" made it their first platinum album, and they even thought briefly about touring again, but the good times didn't roll on. "Hey Nineteen" was the saving grace in their otherwise disappointing follow-up, *Hey Gaucho* (1980). Becker and Fagen had gone their separate ways by 1981, reuniting in 1993 for Fagen's *Kamakiriad*, which led to the unimaginable: a Steely Dan tour in the nineties, and not even with a new record to support.

STYX

The official critics' dartboard band, Styx, with all their falsetto harmonies and pompous art-rock pretensions, sold huge numbers of records in the seventies and early eighties. Critics winced as girls shrieked at the cover-boy looks of guitarist Tommy Shaw, whose high-pitched wail made "Come Sail Away," "Babe," "The Best of Times," and "Too Much Time on My Hands" all top-ten singles. Years later, classic rock radio still finds a place for lofty Styx picks "Renegade," "Grand Illusion," and "Fooling Yourself."

The nucleus of the band, the twin Panozzo brothers, bassist Chuck and drummer John, played with keyboardist Dennis DeYoung and worked the Chicago area as early as 1963. They called themselves Trade Winds, then TW4 before settling on the name Styx, after the mythical river. DeYoung was a music-appreciation teacher familiar with the name. They had their first hit, "Lady," in 1975, which led to an endless stream of hit singles, platinum albums, loads of airplay, and sold-out concert tours. They

Serious rock fans derided their fluff rock, but millions of preteens couldn't get enough of Styx, which included guitarists Tommy Shaw (left) and James Young.

broke up in 1984, but re-formed in 1990 (minus Tommy Shaw, who was replaced by Glenn Burtnick) for *Edge of the Country*.

SUPERTRAMP

Quick—who's the luckiest rocker in history?

Undoubtedly the distinction goes to Rick Davies, the singer and keyboardist of Supertramp, who had his career bankrolled by a well-to-do Dutch millionaire, Stanley August Miesegaes. Legend has it that Miesegaes offered to support Davies' career after seeing him in a band called the Joint. Davies quickly advertised for members, the first initiate being Roger Hodgson, a singer/guitarist, whose prominence in the band was soon equal to that of Davies.

After false starts in the recording studio and a number of less-than-exciting concerts,

Supported by a millionaire patron, Supertramp scored with a series of singles, including "Dreamer," "Bloody Well Right," and "Take the Long Way Home."

Supertramp—the name taken from W.H. Davies' book, *The Autobiography of a Super Tramp*—built a cult following based on solid FM radio airplay, and finally broke through in 1979 with the *Breakfast in America* album and their biggest hit, "The Logical Song." Fat, fluffy rock served ever so politely was Supertramp's recipe, and audiences ate it up. By the end of the seventies, they were one of rock's biggest groups—Miesegaes must have been repaid—but by 1983, Hodgson was history, and the band soon faded, though they continued to record and tour sporadically.

Ted Nugent; Judas Priest's Rob Halford;
Steven Tyler of Aerosmith.

HEAVY METAL THUNDER

Heavy metal, a term first used by William Burroughs in his novel *Naked Lunch*, then repeated in Steppenwolf's "Born to Be Wild," has changed its stripes more than a few times since Burroughs put pen to paper in 1959. Did metal begin in 1964 when the Kinks laid down "You Really Got Me" with Dave Davies new noise contraption, the fuzzbox? Or was it born when Iggy (Pop) and the Stooges made their live debut at a Halloween party in Ann Arbor, Michigan, in October 1967? Maybe Blue Cheer's remake of Eddie Cochran's "Summertime Blues" in 1968 is more to blame. Or London's Deep Purple...or California's Iron Butterfly...or Detroit's MC5...or the ominous Black Sabbath from England's midlands.

Metal evolved along a number of paths through the classic rock years. Like rock, who knows for sure its gristly beginnings? One thing's certain. Heavy metal has taken more heat from parents, lawmakers, rock critics, and nose-in-the-air prims than any other form of rock.

In the eighties and early nineties, it seemed that metalheads like Ozzy Osbourne and Judas Priest were spending more time in the courtroom than the recording studio. Both were brought to trial for allegedly including evil messages in their lyrics. Ozzy was cleared of all charges.

Van Halen had begun the heavy metal renaissance of the late seventies, which peaked in the mid-eighties. But before them, a generous slew of rockers proudly wore the heavy metal banner and tailored their rock for those whose juices flowed just a bit faster than the average rock fan.

AC/DC

Some rock acts spend their entire career reinventing their sound and image. Then there are bands like AC/DC who just keep giving fans what they want: the same song and dance, with absolutely no shame. "People have said we've made the same album thirteen times, but that's a lie," guitarist Angus Young told *Circus* magazine in 1990. "It's been fourteen."

Relentless, hard-driving, pedal-to-the-metal rock delivered a bit tongue-in-cheek is what's on every one of those fourteen albums. At the heart of it since the start have been guitarist Malcolm Young and his little brother Angus. It's not too difficult to distinguish the two. Angus wears the shorts in the family—a schoolboy outfit, that is. In performance he's rarely seen without it.

Angus and Malcolm formed AC/DC in Sydney, Australia, after moving from Glasglow, Scotland. (Their elder brother George was an original member of the Easybeats.) An early version of AC/DC played their first gig in a Sydney bar in December 1973. Months later, sandpaper-throated singer Bon Scott was aboard, as was bassist Mark Evans and drummer Phil Rudd.

Brian Johnson (above) became AC/DC's lead howler in April of 1980, after original singer Bon Scott died following a marathon drinking binge. It was a perfect fit: Johnson didn't sound that much different than Scott.

Their first two albums, *High Voltage* and *TNT*, were released only in Australia, but by 1976, *High Voltage* was available in the States and excitement over the heavy metal band with the schoolboy-suited guitarist was mounting. In 1979, AC/DC broke through to a nationwide audience on the heels of *Highway to Hell*, their first platinum album. But months later, they lost their singer when Bon Scott choked on his own vomit after an all-night drinking binge.

In April 1980, Brian Johnson, sounding nearly identical to Scott, took the front spot, and AC/DC, with no loss of momentum, released another million-seller, *Back in Black*, as arena audiences grew to sold-out proportions. "You Shook Me All Night Long," "For Those About to Rock (We Salute You)," "Dirty Deeds Done Dirt Cheap," and a number of other assaultive rockers continue to wow arena audiences. And Angus still shows up in that schoolboy suit and gives the crowd the same routine, which climaxes each evening with the ceremonial mooning of the audience.

AEROSMITH

They came. They conquered. They pissed it all away. Then they conquered again.

Not many bands win a second chance at superstardom. Aerosmith is the exception. The band from New England couldn't have been more down on their heels in 1982. Joe Perry, having left the group for his own band, was so much in debt that he was living in a Boston boardinghouse. Steven Tyler was holed up in New York in an Eighth Avenue hotel close to the heroin dealers he patronized. Aerosmith was out of vogue and out of luck. Eight of their albums had been released on Columbia, but no more. *Rock in a Hard Place* in 1982 (with guitarist Jimmy Crespo in place of Perry) was the last one they recorded for the label.

But in 1986, an Aerosmith classic, "Walk This Way," a top-ten single from 1975's *Toys in the Attic* album, was revived as a rap-rock hit by Run DMC with vocal assistance by Tyler and Perry, and the band was buzzing again. With the release of *Permanent Vacation* (1987), Aerosmith took a deep breath of a gale-force second wind, which they rode well into the nineties.

It's difficult to call Aerosmith a metal band. Their extravagance stops just short of being lumped in with the big hair and pomposity of most metal outfits. What's more, unlike most metalheads, Aerosmith is in on the joke. Only rarely do they take themselves seriously ("Janie's Got a Gun," for instance). They have always been the perfect mix of sleaze and tease—rhythm and blues–based guitar rock with a lippy, flamboyant singer, a sturdy lead-guitar hero, and a rhythm section that won't let up. Aerosmith just might be rock's greatest party band of all time.

Steven Tyler's resemblance to Mick Jagger and the bands' shared roots in rhythm and blues encouraged comparison with the Rolling Stones.

Steven Tallarico played drums and sang in bands with names like the Strangeurs and Chain Reaction before he met guitarist Anthony Joe Perry at a Sunapee, New Hampshire, ice cream parlor called the Anchorage in the summer of 1970. Tallarico walked and talked like a rock star, and since Perry had his own group, the Jam Band, he invited Tallarico to a gig.

Tallarico was blown away by the Jam Band, and soon he and Perry were jamming with Jam Band bassist Tom Hamilton and thinking of assembling a new outfit. Tallarico brought in two friends, drummer Joey Kramer and guitarist Raymond Tabano, and all five took a three-bedroom apartment at 1325 Commonwealth Avenue in Boston. They lived together, sang together, played together, got high and watched the Three Stooges together, and wrote songs together. Tabano was soon replaced by Brad Whitford, a guitarist who had studied at the Berklee School of Music, as had Kramer. Somewhere along the way, Steven Tallarico became Steven Tyler.

It was Kramer's idea to call their new band Aerosmith. The choice had nothing to do with the Sinclair Lewis novel *Arrowsmith*; Aerosmith was just a word that Kramer had scribbled on his schoolbooks because "it sounded cool." In any event, it was better than the other possibilities— the Hookers and Spike Jones.

The first Aerosmith gig was held at Nimpuc Regional High School in the autumn of 1970. They played cover songs that night—John Lennon's "Cold Turkey," the Stones' "Live with

Me," the Yardbirds' "Shape of Things"—songs they would take with them on their journey to the top. Another Aerosmith tradition was spawned that evening as well—tension between the band members. Tyler argued with Perry about the volume of his guitar; it was the first of many spats.

Aerosmith, the group's first album, was released on Columbia Records in January 1973. Critics immediately slammed the band as Stones clones, but that didn't stop radio stations from airing the stick-out track, "Dream On." When that song was rereleased three years later, it made it to number six on the singles chart. Later that year, "Walk This Way" became their second top-ten single. By 1976 Aerosmith had four albums under their belts and were certified rock stars.

But Perry and Tyler soon became victims of their own indulgences. To them, anything worth doing was worth overdoing. These guys tried anything once, enough to earn them the sobriquet "the toxic twins." It cost them dearly: the band fell apart.In 1979, Perry left to start the Joe Perry Project. Jimmy Crespo replaced him. Whitford, fed up and frustrated, left in 1980.

In the mid-eighties, heavy metal and hard rock began to enjoy a renaissance—it seemed only natural to give one of the originators a second chance. Geffen Records thought so and signed the band, and in 1984, the popular Aerosmith lineup was intact once again. Their first Geffen release, *Done with Mirrors* (1985), was no great shakes, but in 1987, *Permanent Vacation* went multiplatinum. "Dude (Looks Like A Lady)," "Angel," and "Rag Doll" were all top-ten singles. *Pump* (1989) was better yet. Aerosmith, sober and revitalized, was officially back from the grave. Miracles can happen.

BLACK SABBATH

In the early seventies, metal didn't come much darker than the ominous sludge of Black Sabbath. If despairing lyrics and satanic imagery delivered at skull-splitting volume was your cup of blood, you bowed down to Sabbath. This is where heavy metal began to get attached to devil worship, even as all four members insisted that their interest in black magic was a harmless fascination.

Singer John "Ozzy" Osbourne, guitarist Tony Iommi, bassist Terry "Geezer" Butler, and drummer Bill Ward all hailed from Birmingham, England, and first played together in 1968 as Earth. Earth was a pop-rock band influenced by the Move, but when they found out another band was calling itself Earth,

Ozzy Osbourne spent eleven fruitful years as the master of metal macabre with Black Sabbath before embarking on a solo career in 1979.

a name change was necessary. Black Sabbath was chosen based on, depending who you ask, the 1964 Boris Karloff film, or a song Butler wrote, whose title he nicked from a Denis Wheatley novel. They also changed their sound, to heavy hard rock.

Their first album, *Black Sabbath*, was released in 1970, and Sabbath built a devout following that reached a peak in 1974. Four albums in, Sabbath were kings of heavy metal. Ozzy ruled, and fans couldn't get enough of the gloom-'n'-doom stage show, complete with onstage crosses and dark songs like "Paranoid," "Iron Man," "Sabbath Bloody Sabbath," and "War Pigs," all metal classics.

Osbourne left in 1979 to pursue a very successful solo career spearheaded by albums *Blizzard of Ozz* (1980) and *Diary of a Madman* (1981). He was replaced by the elfin Ronnie James Dio. Sabbath kept on through the eighties, but by that point, the bluster came off like a parody.

ALICE COOPER

No, he didn't play Eddie Haskell on *Leave It to Beaver*. That was only a silly rumor, but as rumors go, it was a classic.

Vincent Damon Furnier was Alice Cooper, but sometimes his entire band used the name as well. Alice, of the ghoulish greasepaint, top hat, and cane, was the King of Shock Rock and took rock and roll to new theatrical heights. Who will ever forget the guillotine execution trick? The dismembering of baby dolls? Alice's pet boa constrictor? His stage act might have owed as much to vaudeville as it did to rock, but Alice always cast himself as more of a grand entertainer in the show biz tradition than as a randy rock and roller. Several appearances on the *Hollywood Squares* television show, stints in Las Vegas, Hollywood movie roles, and celebrity golf tournaments with George Burns will attest to that. But make no mistake, Alice rocked. He still does.

Born in Detroit on February 4, 1948, the son of a preacher, Furnier moved to Phoenix when he was a kid and put together his first bands while still in high school. He chose the name Alice Cooper out of the blue and signed to Frank Zappa's record label, Straight, in 1969. His first two albums found a small hard-core following. His third, *Love It to Death*, produced by Bob Ezrin, launched a celebrated career that has lasted well into the nineties.

"Eighteen" was his first single, followed by "School's Out," his first top-ten hit and the catalyst for a string of gold and platinum albums. Fans wore the grooves out of his best albums, *Killer* (1971), *Billion Dollar Babies* (1973), and *Welcome to My Nightmare* (1975). But by the late seventies Cooper faded, as his outrageousness paled in comparison to the punks. After a twelve-year absence from the top-ten charts, Cooper struck in 1989 with "Poison," from the *Trash* album, and has continued touring into the nineties.

Welcome to my nightmare: an Alice Cooper concert almost always included the straitjacket routine, sandwiched somewhere between the guillotine trick and the appearance of Alice's pet boa constrictor.

DEEP PURPLE

Every aspiring guitarist knows the opening power chords to "Smoke on the Water," Deep Purple's signature tune about a concert hall burnt to the ground on the evening of a Frank Zappa concert. (Purple was supposed to record an album there at the same time.) But not many know that Purple's first two hits were cover tunes by Joe South ("Hush") and Neil Diamond ("Kentucky Woman"). The year was 1968, and two years later, Deep Purple's riff-heavy metal broke through to a huge audience.

Deep Purple, formed in 1968 in Hertfordshire, England, considered calling themselves Concrete God but supposedly settled on Deep Purple after guitarist Ritchie Blackmore's grandmother insisted on it. "Deep Purple" was the name of her favorite song, as performed by Nino Tempo and April Stevens.

Purple's first three records were released in America on Tetragrammaton, a small label founded by comedian Bill Cosby. Those early albums were nowhere near as heavy as their 1970 release, *Deep Purple in Rock*. By that time, two of the original members, singer Rod Evans and bassist Nick Semper, had been replaced with Ian Gillan (fresh from *Jesus Christ Superstar*) and Roger Glover, and the mystical rock with which they had begun had been transformed into thick, bone-crunching metal dominated by Blackmore's fat licks. New York heavy rockers Vanilla Fudge were an obvious influence.

Machine Head (1972) was Deep Purple's true breakthrough. With it came "Smoke on the Water" (a number four single) and "Space Truckin'." Progressive FM radio played "Woman From Tokyo," from *Who Do You Think We Are?* (1973), almost as much. But ego problems always plagued Purple. Later that year, David Coverdale was in for Gillan, and Blackmore had left in 1975 to form his own band. Numerous personnel changes continued throughout the seventies, but new lineups could never recapture Purple's glory years. In 1984, Blackmore and Gillan reunited with original keyboardist Jon Lord and drummer Ian Paice for two lackluster records.

> **Deep Purple, who produced heavy metal favorites such as "Speed King" and "Black Night," were designated "loudest rock band" in the *Guinness Book of World Records*.**

GRAND FUNK RAILROAD

Grand Funk Railroad never really played funk, but their straight-ahead, blues-based guitar rock sold astonishing numbers of records in the early seventies. Critics lambasted Grand Funk Railroad before they even pulled out of the station, but continual touring and heavy radio play made up for any bad press.

The band began in Flint, Michigan, as Terry Knight and the Pack, and included guitarist Mark Farner and drummer Don Brewer. Their numerous singles never broke the top forty, but they did set the stage for the band to add bassist Mel Schacher from ? and the Mysterians, change their name to Grand Funk Railroad (a takeoff on Michigan's Grand Trunk Railroad), and land a deal with Capitol Records. Knight became the band's manager.

A loyal fan base began to grow with the release of the first two albums. By the third, *Closer to Home* (1970), they were all over progressive radio with "Closer to Home/I'm Your Captain," and their albums took off. By 1971, their first five records had been certified gold. That year, they sold out two concert dates at New York's Shea Stadium in forty-eight hours, breaking the previous record held by the Beatles.

In 1972, Knight was relieved of his management duties. A string of ugly lawsuits followed, but the band continued to prosper. They officially shortened their moniker to Grand Funk, adopted a more pop sound, and hit the top spot on the singles chart for the first time with the rock anthem "We're an American Band." More top-ten hits continued through the seventies—a new version of Little Eva's "The Loco-Motion," "Some Kind of Wonderful," and "Bad Time"—until they disbanded in 1976. Their last album proper, *Good Singin', Good Playin'*, was produced by Frank Zappa.

IRON BUTTERFLY

Iron Butterfly's seventeen minutes of fame came in the form of "In-A-Gadda-Da-Vida." That's exactly what their big FM radio hit, an extended epic of organ-driven sonic sludge, clocked in at, including the two-and-a-half-minute drum solo. This was heavy stuff for 1968, and rock fans ate up copies of the album of the same title. Three million copies of it were sold before the band's demise in 1971. For a while, Iron Butterfly was the biggest-selling act on the Atco label.

Iron Butterfly was one of the first heavy metal bands, and Doug Ingle was the singer/organist from Nebraska who gave Butterfly its signature sound. In late 1966, he took the band from San Diego to

Iron Butterfly (from left: Erik Braunn, Doug Ingle, Ron Bushy, and Lee Dorman) are the metal pioneers responsible for "In-A-Gadda-Da-Vida."

L.A. and booked gigs at night haunts like the Galaxy and Whisky-A-Go-Go before securing a recording contract.

Because of extensive touring with the Doors and the Jefferson Airplane, Iron Butterfly's 1968 debut, *Heavy*, remained on the album charts for nearly a year. After a lineup adjustment, *In-A-Gadda-Da-Vida* (supposedly translated as "In the Garden of Life") was released and remained on the album charts for 140 weeks, eighty-one of those in the top ten. Another studio album, *Ball*, and a live album followed, but the band made a quick exit and played its farewell performance on May 23, 1971.

JUDAS PRIEST

Next to Ozzy and Sabbath, Judas Priest has taken the most heat from those eager to place blame on heavy metal for supposedly destroying young lives. These accusations sometime make it to the courtroom, as did a case brought against Judas Priest in 1992, in which Priest was charged and found not guilty of recording subliminal messages on their version of Spooky Tooth's "Better by You, Better Than Me." But time after time high-court judges have ruled that, although troubled teens may gravitate to metal (as do millions of well-adjusted kids), the music is not necessarily to blame.

Priest was formed by guitarist K.K. Downing and bassist Ian Hill in Birmingham, England, around 1969. Ear-piercing, dogs-come-runnin' lead howler Rob Halford was in by 1971. After guitarist Glenn Tipton joined in 1974, they released their first album, *Rocka Rolla*. But Priest didn't attract a sizable audience until *British Steel* (1980). In 1982, they finally struck gold with *Screaming for Vengeance*, and followed with the almost-as-heavy *Defenders of the Faith* in 1984. They continued to record and tour into the nineties, but to far less fanfare than in their heyday.

Judas Priest (left, guitarist Glenn Tipton; right, singer Rob Halford), kings of studs and leather, usually began their concerts with Halford's arrival on stage atop his Harley-Davidson.

KISS

It was easy to poke fun at Kiss in 1976. These four characters from New York came off more like comic-book antiheroes than rockers. Kiss was a tough-strut, cock-rock band. They played their instruments crudely. And they wore makeup! What was this—a joke?

Au contraire. Kiss was no joke, just plenty of fun, and they played the game bigger and louder than all the others.

The garish greasepaint immediately set them apart. Then came the elaborate and expensive stage shows, the pyrotechnics, the huge rising drum kits, the blood spitting, the fire breathing, Gene Simmons' mile-long tongue, and the classic albums: *Dressed to Kill*, *Alive*, *Destroyer*. By 1975, the singles were climbing higher. "Beth" went top-ten in 1976. A dry spell struck, even as touring continued, followed by a regular stream of album releases through the eighties into the nineties. And then the inevitable: a torrent of imitators.

For every critic who ever derided Kiss, there are a thousand fans ready to crown Kiss as rock royalty. Through two decades, five personnel changes, a few thousand concert dates, twenty-odd album releases, and more than seventy million records sold, Kiss is still rocking and still loved by millions of fans the world over.

Singer/guitarist Paul Stanley (né Stanley Eisen) had known Gene Simmons (né Chaim Witz before a change to Gene Klein), a bass player and Manhattan schoolteacher, from another band

From left: Gene Simmons, Paul Stanley, and Ace Frehley make up the classic Kiss frontline. Their influence on the legion of hard-rock bands who followed is immeasurable.

before they teamed up and acquired drummer Peter Criss through an ad in *Rolling Stone* magazine. Next aboard was a second guitarist, Ace Frehley, recruited from an ad in the *Village Voice*. Kiss played any Long Island and New York City club that would tolerate their outrageousness. More touring through the Northeast continued, and by 1974, the first Kiss album, on the Casablanca label, was in record stores.

As critics ignored them, fans adored them. There was simply nothing like Kiss: they refused to be photographed or interviewed without their make-up; their concerts were over-the-top, theatrical affairs full of busy stunts; they swore that the red ink used to print a Kiss comic book actually had a fraction of their own blood in it; their fan club, the Kiss Army, was one of rock's most faithful; and there were Kiss lunch boxes, Kiss pinball machines, and even Kiss animated television movies.

There were hits, too. "Rock and Roll All Nite" from *Dressed to Kill* is probably their signature tune. Their biggest hit, "Beth" (1976), was sung by Criss, no longer in the band. (They'll never perform the song live again, they promised Criss.) "Shout It Out Loud," "Hard Luck Woman," "Calling Dr. Love," "Christine Sixteen"—you'll still hear all these at a Kiss concert, and the show will most likely be sold out.

TED NUGENT

Casual rock fans know Ted Nugent as the brash and shrill long-maned, double-talking ax slinger who howls his way through "Cat Scratch Fever"; the Motor City Madman whose mouth is as loud as his guitars; and the gunman and archer who defends his right to bear arms to the end.

He's all that, but Nugent is also a rock and roll journeyman who served for nearly ten years in the psychedelic garage band the Amboy Dukes. Eleven uneven albums with three different labels yielded a modest local following in the Midwest. Their national breakthrough came with the 1968 top-twenty single "Journey to the Center of the Mind," a trippy freak-out with a manic guitar line by Nugent. He was playing guitar as young as age eleven, giving lessons by the time he was sixteen. Most of his time has been spent on the road, playing shows night after night.

Nugent was originally from Detroit, where he played with bands like the Royal High Boys and the Lourds before he moved with his family to Chicago

"If it's too loud you're too old" was the fitting motto of one Ted Nugent tour.

in 1965. He assembled the Amboy Dukes there, remembering the name from a rival Detroit group that had broken up a few years earlier. After a number of nonmonumental albums, they became Ted Nugent and the Amboy Dukes. The name changed, but their luck didn't.

In 1975, Nugent's solo career was on track. He scored a success with *Cat Scratch Fever* (1977). Songs like "Wang Dang Sweet Poontang" and the title track are what the Nuge built the rest of his career on, though he has hardly won many new fans through the eighties. With Tommy Shaw (previously of Styx), Michael Cartelleone on drums, and Jack Blades (ex–Night Ranger) on bass, Nugent formed Damn Yankees in 1989. Offstage, he's a rock journalist's dream. Nugent hunts for his own food, crusades against drugs, and is a strong vocal supporter of gun rights. He'll loudly defend his views at a moment's notice.

STEPPENWOLF

Most bands would trade in their drummer for a shot at recording a song like Steppenwolf's "Born to Be Wild." The perfect rock song if ever there were one, and the one to popularize the phrase "heavy metal thunder," the follow-ups were no duds, either—"Magic Carpet Ride" (1968) and "Rock Me" (1969). Steppenwolf played hard, straight-ahead guitar rock with a certain motorized gusto that made them one of L.A.'s most popular groups in the late sixties.

Singer/guitarist John Kay was born in Tilsit, Germany, and moved to Toronto in 1958 with his family. His first band, Sparrow, a blues-rock outfit, eventually made it to Los Angeles where they

took the name Steppenwolf from the Herman Hesse novel. "Born to Be Wild," from their 1968 self-titled debut album, featured Kay's bravado singing and Goldy McJohn's tasty organ fills. The song made it to number two on the singles chart and appeared on the soundtrack for the classic biker film *Easy Rider*.

After "Rock Me," the top-ten singles dried up, and Steppenwolf showed its political bent on the *Monster* album (1970). Kay even ran for a Los Angeles city council post. By 1972, Kay had embarked on a solo career, and the band called it quits. He attempted to revive the Steppenwolf name in 1974, but by that point, the audience was gone.

VAN HALEN

Van Halen ushered in the heavy metal renaissance of the eighties, but the boys from Pasadena, California, started woodshedding as early as 1974. Since 1978, they have scored hit after hit. Their albums consistently chart in the top thirty. In the mid-nineties, they show no signs of slowing down.

Guitarist Edward Van Halen, the Wizard of Ax, is that rare specimen among modern-day guitarists: a true originator. He tagged his own chapter on to the Page-Beck-Clapton-Hendrix handbook of electric-guitar playing, patenting his own style of hammer-ons, pull-offs, two-handed neck-tapping, and other guitar tricks. He took piano lessons as a kid, as did his older brother Alex, but then moved on to drums. Alex acquired a guitar and learned how to play it.

But in Edward's hands, Alex's guitar really sang. In time, Eddie was playing the guitar and Alex the drums. With Michael Anthony on bass, they started a band called Mammoth. A few months later, flashy singer David Lee Roth was aboard and the band changed their name to Van Halen.

David Lee Roth (left, with guitar wiz Eddie Van Halen), a consummate showman, attracted a loyal following with his flamboyant vocal style and onstage antics.

The early Van Halen played cover material by the Kinks, Roy Orbison, and Martha and the Vandellas on the southern California bar circuits before adding original songs. In 1977, they landed a record deal with Warner Bros. and had their first disc in stores by the next year. The album, *Van Halen*, went multiplatinum and broke the top twenty as their tours, highlighted by Van Halen's guitar pyrotechnics and Roth's swaggering persona, became sellouts.

Six albums later, Van Halen upped the ante with *1984*. Eddie added synthesizer bits and the band became more pop. They scored their first number one hit ("Jump") and their audience multiplied. In 1985, Roth announced his departure, and Van Halen added singer Sammy Hagar, with his shrill voice and Shirley Temple ringlets, who came from the mediocre rock band Montrose.

Roth's solo career took a turn toward vaudeville—he covered a Louis Prima song on his first EP—and was quite successful, but he has mentioned in interviews that he would welcome a reunion of the original Van Halen lineup. The band, however, seems perfectly content with Hagar.

CLEAR VOICES

As the seventies drew to a close, a small number of rock musicians emerged as spokespersons for the classic rock era. Most never asked for such a lofty mantle, but they rose to superstardom nonetheless, inspiring millions with their distinct messages. They simply used rock music to convey some stronger signal.

Many were survivors of an earlier era. Eric Clapton, John Lennon, Paul McCartney, Rod Stewart, and Neil Young all played in one huge band or another in the sixties. It's a good bet that their individual talents would have emerged no matter who else played in their respective bands. Paul Simon had recorded as early as 1957 and Stevie Wonder had begun his long recording career in 1963. Boz Scaggs paid his dues with the Steve Miller Band, Todd Rundgren with the Nazz, and Lou Reed with the Velvet Underground. Elton John and Bob Seger both released their debut albums in 1969.

Others came later to the dance. The debut album from Bruce Springsteen didn't arrive until 1972; Billy Joel released his breakthrough, *Piano Man*, in 1973; Tom Petty kicked off his long, fruitful career in 1976. The last bona fide rock stars to emerge from the seventies, these three were the first of a breed of rockers to hail the sixties as an influential period. Springsteen cited Bob Dylan and Roy Orbison as key influences, while the sound of his 1975 opus *Born to Run* owes a debt to the Phil Spector "wall of sound" productions—the Ronettes, the Righteous Brothers, Darlene Love—from the mid-sixties. Billy Joel, in his youth, listened to Fats Domino and Jerry Lee Lewis records for hours on end.

Rock and roll had come full circle and was poised to explode in a million new directions. The clear voices of the seventies represent the end of an era—a time before MTV, when the only place to see performers was in concert, a time when a singer on stage lent an aura of romance to rock and roll.

John Lennon; Eric Clapton; Bruce Springsteen.

ERIC CLAPTON

"Clapton is God!" the fans spray-painted on the walls of London's tube stations. In spite of the hype, few people will disagree that Eric Clapton knows his way around a six-stringed fretboard like no other ax shredder.

Born in Ripley, England, on March 30, 1945, Clapton was influenced by bluesmen Robert Johnson, Muddy Waters, Elmore James, and Willie Dixon via the guitar work of Alexis Korner. Clapton started playing when he was seventeen and was in his first band, the Roosters, by 1963. He went on to the Yardbirds until 1965, then John Mayall's bluesbreakers. He formed Cream in 1966 with Jack Bruce and Ginger Baker, then went on to Blind Faith in 1968. In 1970, he formed Derek and the Dominoes. After two years of seclusion—a dreadful heroin-plagued period of his life—he performed his renowned comeback concert at London's Rainbow Theatre in January 1973.

The long, storied career of Eric Clapton began on the streets of England's Kingston and Richmond, where he paid his dues as a sidewalk musician before joining his first band, the Roosters. From there, he joined a series of bands, ultimately settling into a strong career as a solo artist.

He was back with a vengeance with *461 Ocean Boulevard* (1974), an album many fans consider his best work.

Others might cite *Slow-hand* as his best. Released in 1977, the album scored with "Wonderful Tonight," "Lay Down Sally," and a reading of J.J. Cale's "Cocaine." Here Clapton showed that his sweet voice was as effective as his stellar guitar playing.

There are many Clapton compilations, but fans looking for a Clapton primer are directed to *Timepieces*, Volumes I and II (1982), as well as *Crossroads* (1988), an all-encompassing seventy-three-song retrospective. Not to mention the Derek and the Dominoes boxed sets. His work through the eighties stayed on a steady plane with *Money and Cigarettes* (1983) and *Journeymen* (1989). By the nineties, he was enjoying yet another renaissance with his *MTV Unplugged* album, featuring "Tears in Heaven" written for his late son, and an acoustic version of "Layla," probably his most popular song.

BILLY JOEL

Crooning at the grand piano—affirming his affection for a loved one or articulating the shortcomings of the entertainer's life—is where Billy Joel has always seemed most at home. The cherub-faced singer has never been entirely comfortable with this image. At times, he has tried to combine his soft, sit-down balladeer persona with a tough-guy stance. Sometimes the mix works ("Uptown Girl" in 1983, "A Matter of Trust" in 1986). At other times it seems contrived. Still, Billy Joel, smarmy and successful in sneakers and a necktie, has sold millions of records and packs arenas wherever he plays.

A native Long Islander, he was born William Martin Joel on May 9, 1949. He took piano lessons as a kid, and later fell in with a suburban street gang of toughs who called themselves the Parkway Green Gang. During 1964's British Invasion, the rock and roll bug bit Billy, and he formed the Echoes, who became the Emerald Lords, then the Lost Souls. They were all the rage at Hicksville High, where Joel himself, a troubled teenager, was persona non grata; he was denied graduation with the class of 1967 because of his lack of credits. He ran away from home and spent a night in the pokey on suspicion of burglary charges after cops found him loitering on the front stoop of a house.

Joel joined the Hassles, a group that recorded two albums, *The Hassles* and *Hour of the Wolf*, for United Artists Records before calling it quits. Joel's longtime girlfriend bailed out on him at this point and he battled severe depression. Following a suicide attempt, he committed himself to the mental ward of Meadowbrook Hospital in East Meadow, Long Island, for a brief stay.

Native Long Islander Billy Joel cut his eyeteeth in a greaser band called the Hassles. His solo career didn't take root until 1972, when he moved to L.A. and played piano bars under the name Bill Martin.

His next band was called Attila, a two-man psychedelic outfit with Hassles drummer Jon Small, but that didn't pan out, either. His first solo album, *Cold Spring Harbor* (1972), was poorly executed; Joel sounded like he was breathing helium. He hightailed it to Los Angeles to try his luck on the West Coast and played bars under the name Bill Martin. Here was the setting for his first top-forty single, "Piano Man."

Within a year, Joel had a contract with the Columbia label, his *Piano Man* record landed in stores, and his career finally began to bloom. He gained momentum with every release and reached a high point in 1977 with *The Stranger*, his biggest-selling album to date. From there on, Joel could do no wrong. From 1977 to 1986, Billy Joel racked up twenty-eight top-forty singles, seven of those top tens, two of those—"It's Still Rock and Roll to Me" (1980) and "Tell Her About It" (1983)—number ones. His albums went multiplatinum. His music appealed to everyone from school kids to the VH-1 generation. Even Frank Sinatra sang Joel's "New York State of Mind."

In the mid-eighties, Joel was making headlines more because of his marriage to model Christie Brinkley (from whom he is now divorced) than for his music, but he was still as popular as ever. He has made the east end of Long Island his permanent home, and has been a fierce fighter for the rights of the local baymen.

ELTON JOHN

He was classic rock's own Liberace. Just about everything that singer/music writer/piano virtuoso Elton John touched in the seventies turned to gold. No fewer than twenty-four of his singles hit the top forty. Most of his eighteen albums released during the decade sold more than a million each. Not bad for a guy who seems an unlikely figure for a rock star. Gap-toothed, balding, and forever fighting a paunch, he's still a stout, bouncy ball of energy onstage, even if his act is nowhere near as flamboyant as it was in the seventies.

He was born Reginald Kenneth Dwight on March 25, 1947, in Pinner, England, but he knew that name wouldn't be glamorous enough for the elaborate career he was planning. While playing with a band called Bluesology, which he joined at age eighteen, he answered an ad looking for new talent as Elton John, taking the first names of Bluesology sax player Elton Dean and singer John Baldry.

Elton could write the music, but not the lyrics. Bernie Taupin, however, could. He answered that same ad, began collaborating with Elton—first on easy-listening tunes for others, then rockers for Elton—and became just as important a part of Elton John's career as the hundreds of eyeglasses, platform heels, pink feather boas, and extravagant costumes he wore on stage.

The songs covered the gamut from unrequited love swoons to gospel-flavored ballads to fifties-style crewcut rock to points beyond. Classical excursions and a fair share of studio experiments informed their records, but what was particularly interesting was Taupin and John's modus operandi. They rarely worked in each other's company. Taupin sent lyrics to John, and John tied them to music. This hit factory chugged out hit after hit from 1970 into the nineties. When Taupin was away from the scene in the late seventies, John's career suffered.

His first American album, *Elton John*, set a chart-scaling, record-breaking career in swing that would last a lifetime. After the poignant "Your Song," his first single, reached the top ten in late 1970, he was back two years later with "Rocket Man," then "Honky Cat," "Daniel," and his first number one hit, "Crocodile Rock." The hits kept comin', as did the platinum albums that spawned them: most notably *Tumbleweed Connection* (1971), *Honky Chateau* (1972), *Goodbye Yellow Brick Road* (1973), *Captain Fantastic and the Brown Dirt Cowboy* (1975), and his hardest-rocking album, *Rock of the Westies* (1975). His concerts have been sellouts since he started. He was the first Western rocker to tour the former Soviet Union.

An avid record collector, rock and rhythm and blues lover, social activist, infrequent thespian (he was the Pinball Wizard in the film version of *Tommy*), and tireless performer, John is as much at home singing a duet with Jennifer Rush or Dionne Warwick as he is kicking over the piano stool during the third encore. Although his flash has faded, Elton John is a career artist who will make records for as long as he wants.

Which was bigger? The flamboyant Elton John's string of unstoppable hits—or his wardrobe trunks stuffed with specialty eyeglasses and feathered costumes?

JOHN LENNON

The first Beatle to record outside the group, John Lennon recorded a string of top-forty hits and critically well received albums on his own that stand up with rock's finest. Many of them, recorded with his second wife, Yoko Ono, showed that Lennon's pen clearly had not run out of ink when the Beatles dissolved in 1970. Lennon was a crusader for peace and civil rights, and a fierce believer in the importance of personal independence; he used his gift for songwriting to pursue this agenda until his final hours. His brutal murder on December 8, 1980, marked rock and roll's saddest day.

His antiwar anthem "Give Peace a Chance," recorded in 1969 in a Canadian hotel suite, was credited to the Plastic Ono Band. Next came "Cold Turkey," and then the Beatles split. Lennon's first album, *John Lennon–Plastic Ono Band*, which he coproduced with Ono and Phil Spector, yielded not a single hit, but Beatles fans heard one of Lennon's most beautiful songs, "Love."

His next album, *Imagine* (1971), displayed Lennon at his most insightful in the title track, but also at his nastiest in the song "How Do You Sleep?" It was a stinging attack on McCartney, perhaps in retaliation for two songs on McCartney's *Ram* album, "Too Many People" and "Back Seat of My Car." Some called his next records—*Some Time in New York City* (with Yoko), *Mind Games*, and *Walls and Bridges*—uneven, but *Walls* included the number one single "Whatever Gets You Thru the Night," a duet with Elton John. On *Rock 'n' Roll* (1975), Lennon paid

John Lennon met Japanese artist Yoko Ono in 1966 and married her three years later, on March 20, 1969. The artistic inspiration he could no longer extract from the mop-tops was readily drawn from the couple's tight-knit relationship.

his respects to his favorite rock 'n' rollers of the past—Fats Domino, Ben E. King, Sam Cooke, Little Richard, and others—and recorded an album of straight cover songs.

Lennon fought deportation from the U.S. through the early seventies and was finally granted a permanent visa in July 1976. By then he and Ono had taken up residence at the Dakota, a historic apartment building on the corner of Central Park West and West 72nd Street in Manhattan, and had found solace in their long walks in the park.

In August 1980, Lennon and Ono began work on their first record in six years, the exquisite *Double Fantasy*. The album, released on November 17, included "Starting Over," a number one single that seemed to point the couple in a fresh direction. But three weeks later, as he was returning home from the recording studio, Lennon was shot in the archway of the Dakota by a deranged gunman who inquired "Mr. Lennon?" before opening fire. Lennon staggered up six steps to the office of Jay Hastings and uttered his last words, "I'm shot. I'm shot." He was rushed to Roosevelt Hospital, where he died from a massive loss of blood.

Lennon was cremated at Hartsdale Crematorium in New York State, and fans held a vigil in front of the Dakota for two gray days. Ono issued a short statement: "John loved and prayed for the human race. Please do the same for him."

PAUL McCARTNEY

Paul McCartney, like his mop-top counterpart, John Lennon, set his solo career wheels in motion while still with the Beatles. *McCartney* (1970), his first solo disc, which contained the international hit "Maybe I'm Amazed," was full of pleasing pop and was a definite harbinger of things to come from the cute Beatle.

With wife Linda sharing a credit, McCartney released his next album, *Ram* (1971), which included his first solo number one hit, "Uncle Albert/Admiral Halsey." McCartney topped the singles charts all through the seventies with hits like "My Love" (1973), "Listen to What the Man Said" (1975), "Silly Love Songs" (1976), and "With a Little Luck" (1978).

He formed Wings in 1971 with Linda on keyboards, ex–Moody Blues guitarist Denny Laine, and Denny Seiwell on drums. In 1972, guitarist Henry McCullough joined but was gone the next year, replaced by ex–Thunderclap Newman guitarist James McCulloch.

McCartney has taken his knocks over the years, especially over the questionable talents of his wife. But that didn't keep fans from buying albums like *Band on the Run* (1973), *Venus and Mars* (1975), and *Tug of War* (1982). Although Wings officially disbanded in April 1981, McCartney continued to release albums throughout the eighties and into the nineties.

After the Beatles split, Paul McCartney rarely performed in public without his wife, Linda.

TOM PETTY AND THE HEARTBREAKERS

It's a good bet that Tom Petty's collection has every Byrds record ever released. Sometimes his sneering, nasal voice is a dead ringer for Roger McGuinn's. And Petty makes his twelve-string guitar ring just as resoundingly as the Byrds did theirs. But he's much more than a copycat act. Petty's rock and roll stands on its own for its widely accessible songs about unrequited love and fractured relationships. His sonic connection to popular sixties rock from harmony-rich artists like the Byrds and the Searchers hasn't hurt, either.

Petty, born in Gainesville, Florida, on October 20, 1953, played in a group called the Epics while he was still in high school. At seventeen, he joined popular Florida band Mudcrutch and played next to guitarist Mike Campbell and keyboardist Benmont Tench, who would later join him in the Heartbreakers. By the early seventies, Petty was in L.A. and had himself a deal with Shelter Records.

Florida native Tom Petty has had a long and varied career, including membership in one of rock's latest supergroups, the Traveling Wilburys.

In 1975, Petty heard a demo that Campbell and Tench had worked on with bassist Ron Blair and drummer Stan Lynch, and it was decided that all five would take a shot in the recording studio. That first record, *Tom Petty and the Heartbreakers*, was released in 1976. Although it initially sold poorly, constant touring and a cult base in England finally translated to success in the U.S. Petty's first single, "Breakdown," was rereleased a year after the album first hit, and climbed all the way to number forty.

Through the years, Petty's appearance changed with his sound. Tight leather outfits eventually gave way to a more casual jacket-and-jeans look. By the end of the seventies, he was regarded as a major act as his third album, *Damn the Torpedoes*, climbed all the way to number two on the charts and sold three million copies on the strength of "Refugee" and "Don't Do Me Like That." He continues to write, record, and tour into the nineties.

LOU REED

Lou Reed is New York City. Just as the Beach Boys embody the sound of southern California and ZZ Top's guitar boogie does the same for the state of Texas, Reed's songs have always dealt with the dark side of the city's landscape. He is classic rock's ghetto poet, offering tales about Bowery dwellers, transvestites, kinky sex, drug addiction, suicide, homicide, and so on. He's never sold huge numbers of records, but Lou Reed is that rare original talent. His influence is immeasurable; in large part, he laid the groundwork for punk rock.

Born Louis Firbank on March 2, 1944, Reed was a proficient poet and songwriter in his youth. He attended Syracuse University and was in New York's Greenwich Village by the mid-sixties playing in a band called the Primitives, which would one day be called the Velvet Underground. With John Cale, Sterling Morrison, Maureen Tucker, and, for a brief spell, singer/model Nico, the Velvet Underground recorded only four albums during their short career. VU songs "Sweet Jane," "Rock and Roll," "Waiting for the Man," and "Heroin" are considered classics by critics, even if radio airplay has been marginal.

Lou Reed: the sound of New York City.

Reed left the Velvets in 1970 after a summer-long stint at the renowned Max's Kansas City nightclub and dropped out of the rock scene until two years later, when he released his first solo album and the follow-up breakthrough, *Transformer*. The album's most memorable song, "Walk on the Wild Side," an ode to the outcasts who populated the films of director Andy Warhol, became Reed's only top-twenty single. The song set a twenty-plus album career in motion—marked by classics like *Rock 'n' Roll Animal* (1974), *Coney Island Baby* (1976), *The Bells* (1979), *The Blue Mask* (1982), and *New York* (1989)—which would last well into the nineties.

TODD RUNDGREN

Singer/songwriter/accomplished guitarist/production wizard Todd Rundgren has never been content with just one job. He has been involved with so many different projects that it's impossible to nail him down to one specific style. With his early band, the Nazz, his songs were structured in catchy Beatlesque pop. With Runt and on his own he continued on that course but included more experimental adventures. With Utopia he jumped into complex progessive rock. And he produced pivotal albums for Patti Smith, the Tubes, the New York Dolls, Grand Funk Railroad, Badfinger, Meat Loaf, and many others. And he is always on the cutting edge when it comes to new technologies, such as CD-ROM and interactive video.

In Upper Darby, Pennsylvania, Rundgren played in a high school outfit called Money and with a Philadelphia blues band called Woody's Truckstop before starting his first serious outfit, the Nazz. The were highly acclaimed, but their four-album catalog of bouncy rock-pop never made it out of the Philadelphia area. One of their best tunes, "Hello It's Me," became a number five hit for Rundgren later in his career, in 1973.

Rundgren scored his first hit, "We Gotta Get You a Woman," in 1970 with his next band, Runt. Two years later, he released what many fans feel is his masterwork, the double-disc *Something/Anything*. Playing nearly all the instruments himself and overdubbing layers of vocals, the album was a pop-rock fan's dream and included Todd's second top-forty single, "I Saw the Light."

Rundgren's fan base didn't increase through the late seventies or eighties. The hit singles dried up as critics accused him of self-indulgence. Still, fans bought up copies of *Faithful* in 1976 and *Hermit of Mink Hollow* in 1978. His trippy hard-rock band, Utopia, put out eight albums and mustered one hit single, "Set Me Free," but not many memorable songs.

An inveterate experimenter, Todd Rundgren has produced dozens of pivotal albums, as well as starred in his own one-man band and with his group Utopia.

A wizard at the production board, Rundgren built his own computer-video studio in Woodstock, New York, in 1981 and has always been considered a leader in pioneering new technologies. As the information superhighway stretches further across America into the nineties, no doubt Rundgren will be at the musical forefront.

BOZ SCAGGS

He's been exiled to the "Whatever Happened To...?" columns, but in the late seventies, soulful singer/songwriter/guitarist Boz Scaggs was a serious contender in the competitive arena of white-boy blues-rock and assembled a string of hit singles alongside an impressive number of critically received albums. A master at the she-left-me, baby-come-back school of songcraft, his *Silk Degrees* album is considered a classic.

Boz was born William Royce Scaggs on June 8, 1944, in Ohio. A longtime sidekick of Steve Miller, Scaggs embarked on a solo career in 1969 with a strong American debut album coproduced by *Rolling Stone* magazine editor Jann Wenner. With Duane "Skydog" Allman on hand to provide the thrills with his sly Dobro and guitar fills, the debut was a favorite among critics but hardly a hit with fans. Scaggs didn't attract serious attention until *Silk Degrees* hit in 1976 with two major hits, "Low-down" and "Lido Shuffle." Later releases could never match *Degrees*, however. He was almost nowhere to be found in the eighties, except for a 1988 release, *Other Roads*.

Above: Boz Scaggs released the classic *Silk Degrees* LP in 1976. Right: Bob Seger racked up eighteen top-twenty singles between 1969 and 1987.

BOB SEGER

It took nearly the entire decade of the sixties for Bob Seger to build a following in the Detroit area. He finally gained national recognition in 1969 with "Ramblin' Gamblin' Man," but it was another seven years before Seger's straight-ahead, guitar-based, blue-collar rock found a huge audience. Seger never forgot his roots. There was never anything glitzy or glamorous about him, and he didn't have to change his act to become popular.

The son of a big-bandleader, Seger played in a variety of bar bands and racked up a few local Detroit hits in the sixties before signing with Capitol Records in 1969. Seven albums later, Seger was still searching for that big national hit. He finally got it in 1976 with "Night Moves" from the album of the same name, and Bob Seger and the Silver Bullet Band never looked back. "Still the Same," "Hollywood Nights," "We've Got Tonite," "Fire Lake," "Against the Wind," and "Tryin' to Live My Life Without You" were all top-twenty hits as "Feel Like A Number," "Old Time Rock and Roll," and "Rock and Roll Never Forgets" were played endlessly on album-oriented FM radio stations. He released ten albums from 1972 to 1982, all critically well received, and continued to record into the nineties.

A heartland rocker in the mold of Bruce Springsteen, John Mellencamp, and Tom Petty, Seger is living proof that hard work and determination pay off.

PAUL SIMON

Fans of Paul Simon might hold the songs he recorded with Art Garfunkel closer to their hearts than any of his solo tunes. Still, he's been recording on his own for twenty-five years, five times as long as his period with Garfunkel, and his solo career has certainly overstepped the boundaries of folk rock. Rhymin' Simon added reggae, calypso, and African rhythms to his introspective lyrics, acoustic guitar chords, and winsome voice to forge a unique style of world music.

Paul Simon's solo career continues the commercial and critical success he first earned with former partner Art Garfunkel.

The eclecticism began as soon as he parted ways with Garfunkel in 1970. The reggae-flavored "Mother and Child Reunion," from his 1972 solo debut album, was his first hit and a hint of where he was heading. His second release, *There Goes Rhymin' Simon* (1973), featured singers the Dixie Hummingbirds and the Peruvian group Urubamba, and contained top-five hits "Kodachrome" and "Loves Me Like a Rock." Many Simon fans say his 1975 release, *Still Crazy After All These Years*, is his best. Others point to *Graceland* (1986). African rhythms complemented his folk-based songs—"You Can Call Me Al," "The Boy in the Bubble," "Graceland"—perfectly. It was a welcome rebound from two lackluster efforts, *Hearts and Bones* (1983) and *One Trick Pony* (1980), the latter also a movie that Simon wrote and in which he appeared. It was no *Annie Hall* (the 1977 Woody Allen film that Simon had a small role in).

Simon has never completely called it quits with Garfunkel. They continue to appear sporadically in record and in performance. It's a good bet that they will record another album together before the century's out. The harmony is just too perfect.

BRUCE SPRINGSTEEN

They're not booing. They're yelling, "BRUUUUUCE!"

For millions of fans, Bruce Springsteen is the Boss. (His longtime group, the E Street Band, dubbed him that whenever it was time to get paid.) He represents all of what rock and roll promised in its infancy: freedom, salvation, deliverance from oppression, power through music. Springsteen is street poet, rugged singer, able guitarist, occasional pianist, charismatic front man, ardent rock and roll fan, and, most of all, rock's most consummate showman. Ask Bruce where he fits in the rock pantheon and he'll probably answer with the credo that has closed so many of his marathon concerts: "I'm just a prisoner of rock and roll."

He's also New Jersey's most popular musical export, next to Frank Sinatra. On September 23, 1949, the first child of Adele and Douglas Springsteen was born in Freehold, New Jersey. Young Bruce listened to AM radio for hours on end and fell in love with the music of Roy Orbison, Gary U.S. Bonds, the Phil Spector productions (Ronettes, Darlene Love), Chuck Berry, and the Beatles. At age nine he saw Elvis Presley on *The Ed Sullivan Show* and was immediately hooked. His mom bought him a guitar, but his left hand was too small to wrap around the fretboard, so into the closet it went. Five years later he gave the guitar another try.

Bruce taught himself licks off the singles he purchased at the local record shop and was in his first band, the Castiles, by the time he was sixteen. After high school graduation, he joined Earth, a power trio in the style of Cream, and began hanging out in Asbury Park, New Jersey.

Next came Steel Mill, with organist Danny Federici and drummer/ex-convict Vini "Mad Dog" Lopez, both future E Streeters.

Bruce Springsteen parlayed stinging guitar licks, rich keyboard fills, romantic poetry, basic rock rhythms, and an affinity for tall rock and roll tales into the quintessential Jersey Shore sound.

Here Bruce expanded his range, singing lead vocals on Martha Reeves' "Dancin' in the Streets" and Steel Mill originals like "Sister Theresa," "Goin' Back to Georgia," and "Resurrection." After a short tour of California, they returned east and added "Miami" Steve Van Zandt on bass guitar.

Steel Mill closed shop in 1971, and Springsteen started Dr. Zoom and the Sonic Boom. They played only three dates, one an opening stint with the Allman Brothers, but it was Bruce's biggest and craziest band ever: a horn section, background singers, and, oddly, a Monopoly game board set up center stage. Next came the Bruce Springsteen Band with Van Zandt moving to guitar, bassist Garry W. Tallent, Lopez, and pianist/guitarist David Sancious. There was also a horn section at first, but after Bruce met saxophonist Clarence Clemons (a fateful encounter he's retold many times during the introduction to the slow concert version of "The E Street Shuffle"), he dumped the horns and hired "The Big Man." Bruce's songwriting improved. Although audiences fell in love with originals like "I Just Can't Change" and "The Band's Just Boppin' the Blues," Bruce disbanded the group in autumn 1971 and took a stab at a solo career.

He met Mike Appel the next year and hired him as manager, but foolishly signed a long-term deal one evening on an automobile hood in an unlit parking lot. It was a lopsided, losing agreement that Springsteen would later regret and try to sever in court. But Appel did bring Bruce to the attention of Columbia Records executive John Hammond, the man who signed Bob Dylan and Billie Holiday. Apparently, Appel marched Bruce into Hammond's office and wouldn't shut up about this great new talent. Bruce finally played a few songs for Hammond right there in the office, on piano, not guitar. After Hammond heard "If I Were the Priest," a song Bruce has never officially released, Hammond put the wheels in motion that would bring Bruce to Columbia.

Bruce's first record, *Greetings from Asbury Park, New Jersey*, in stores by January 1973, didn't set any sales records, but it brought the group back together. Somewhere along the way, Bruce started calling them the E Street Band, and his cult following grew larger. They played any club that would have them. (A brief, ill-received arena tour supporting Chicago convinced him not to open for other bands, and to stick to clubs and theaters.)

The Wild, the Innocent and the E Street Shuffle came next, which included the song Bruce would close many concerts with, the exhilarating "Rosalita," and the buzz grew louder. Rock critic Jon Landau wrote a rave review in *The Real Paper*, saying, "I saw rock and roll's future and its name is Bruce Springsteen," and wound up not only replacing Appel as Bruce's manager but coproducing his next record, *Born to Run*. The album took a long time to complete; Bruce agonized over capturing the proper sound. When the record was finally released in October 1975, Columbia's hype machine almost spun out of control. Bruce was heralded not only as the new Dylan, but as a rock messiah, and landed on the covers of both *Time* and *Newsweek* in the same week. He added Max Weinberg on drums and Roy Bittan on piano, but lengthy legal battles resulting in a court injunction brought by Appel prevented Bruce from releasing any more records until 1978.

Springsteen was playing arenas by the time *Darkness on the Edge of Town* was finally released. His concerts stretched to three hours with an intermission and no opening act. His voice grew huskier as his writing turned less romantic and more concerned about the hardships of the working man. His songs became hits for Manfred Mann ("Blinded by the Light," a number one single), Robert Gordon ("Fire," later recorded by the Pointer Sisters), and Patti Smith (the gorgeous "Because the Night"). *The River* (1980), a double-disc set, brought him his first top-ten single in the bouncy "Hungry Heart," and Bruce toured worldwide, selling out concerts in Japan and Australia.

Saxophonist Clarence Clemons (right) was the perfect foil for Springsteen's rock lore.

It seemed Bruce had reached his summit, but his biggest seller was yet to come. After an acoustic sidetrip, *Nebraska*, Springsteen let loose in 1984 with *Born in the U.S.A.* The title track, a Vietnam veteran's painful remembrance, was misinterpreted by many as a sort of patriotic cheer. The album spawned a remarkable seven top-ten singles and has sold more than twelve million copies to date. It made Bruce a redoubtable rock icon. To satisfy the overwhelming number of fans, he added stadiums to the arena tour. Guitarist Nils Lofgren replaced Van Zandt, and Bruce invited background singer Patti Scialfa, the first female E Streeter since violinist Suki Lahov in the early seventies. Bruce later married Scialfa, after divorcing model/actress Julianne Phillips.

What next but a live album? *Live 1975–1985*, a five-record set, spanned most of Bruce's career and confirmed that a Bruce Springsteen and the E Street Band gig was the show against which all other rock concerts were measured. But it was his last album with all the E Streeters. His next record, the somber *Tunnel of Love* (1987), included just a fragment of his beloved group.

But the E Street Band was all in tow for the *Tunnel of Love* tour, another worldwide affair. The next year, Bruce and the E Streeters supported the *Human Rights Now* tour for Amnesty International. Sadly, it was the final ride for the E Street Band. During the inactivity of the next two years, the band went their separate ways, at Bruce's suggestion. Some speculated that bad blood had splintered the group, but Bruce's desire to experiment with new musicians was the true culprit. His next record and tour for *Human Touch* and *Lucky Town*, both CDs released simultaneously, included a group of no-names except for Bittan.

ROD STEWART

Rod Stewart had been in so many bands before striking out on his own, success was inevitable. Rod the Mod's raspy voice is one of rock's most recognizable, and he's used it to cover songs by Tom Waits, Cat Stevens, and Bob Dylan, as well as for his own compositions.

Stewart, born in London on January 10, 1945, was a soccer lover who had aspirations to play the sport, but he ended up only warming the bench as an apprentice with a pro team. Music was his salvation. He played harmonica with Jimmy Powell and the Five Dimensions and sang with the Hoochie Coochie Men, a band called Steampacket (with Brian Auger), and a group called Shotgun Express before teaming with the Jeff Beck Group in 1967. Two years later, his first solo release, *The Rod Stewart Album*, was in stores, and Rod split his career equally between the solo discs and as front man for the Faces.

His haggard, sandpaper voice seemed perfectly matched to the blues songs he covered (the Stones' "Street Fightin' Man," Ewan MacColl's "Dirty Old Town") and the early ones he wrote ("Cindy's Lament," "An Old Raincoat Won't Ever Let You Down"). His first solo single, a song he cowrote called "Maggie May," climbed straight to number one in 1971, as did the album it came from, *Every Picture Tells a Story*, regarded by many as his masterpiece.

Rod Stewart fronted the Jeff Beck Group and the Faces on the way to establishing himself as a solid solo performer. His three biggest hits were "Maggie May" in 1971, "Tonight's the Night" in 1976 and "Da Ya Think I'm Sexy?" in 1978.

Through the seventies, into the eighties, and beyond, Stewart consistently returned to the top of the charts with hit after hit. "Tonight's the Night," "You're in My Heart," "Da Ya Think I'm Sexy?" "Passion," and "Young Turks" all reached the top five and Stewart—balladeer, showman, ladies' man—seemed indestructible.

STEVIE WONDER

The sixteen Grammy awards he has received give some indication of the depth of Stevie Wonder's talent. Since 1963, Wonder has released forty-five top-forty singles, an astonishing number. Many of his twenty-seven albums have been million-sellers. He continually expands his sound, forever experimenting with new instruments and rhythms. And he has done it all without the gift of sight.

Wonder was born Steveland Morris on May 15, 1950, in Saginaw, Michigan. Blind since birth, he was recording for the Motown label as Little Stevie Wonder in 1963 when his "Fingertips (Part 2)" climbed all the way to number one. He played harmonica on his first hit, and was soon writing and singing favorites like "Uptight (Everything's Alright)," "I Was Made to Love Her," "For Once in My Life," "My Cherie Amour," "Signed, Sealed, Delivered I'm Yours," and "If You Really Love Me."

But Wonder is more than a singles artist. Beginning with *Music of My Mind* (1972), Wonder's albums grew in scope. He wrote, produced, and played most of the instruments on chartbusters like *Talking Book* (1972); *Innervisions* (1973), which included the chilling "Living for the City"; *Fulfillingness' First Finale* (1974); and his tour de force, *Songs in the Key of Life* (1976). These records covered all of pop's bases: reggae, soul, blues, rhythm and blues, and rock.

Wonder's output slowed in the late eighties and early nineties, but he has already contributed enough to give him a permanent place in popular music.

Stevie Wonder was only thirteen years old when his first hit single, "Fingertips (Part 2)," climbed to number one.

NEIL YOUNG

How fitting that a book on classic rock closes with the man who transcends generations like no other rocker. While so many has-beens from the sixties and seventies come off like tired dinosaurs, Neil Young soldiers on with as much honor and purpose as in his days with Buffalo Springfield. He's a genuine rocker who still has a long way to go before running out of gas.

Sweet singer, insightful songwriter, blistering guitarist, and toy-train collector Neil Young has never been content to stay in one mold. He's rocked with Crazy Horse and Booker T. and the MG's, exchanged country laments with Willie Nelson and Waylon Jennings, harmonized with James Taylor and Linda Ronstadt, ripped it up with Pearl Jam—and he devoted a number of years to collaboration with Crosby, Stills and Nash. He's been called the Godfather of Grunge, the original punk.

Born November 12, 1945, in Toronto, Canada, Neil played in early bands called the Squires and the Mynah Birds, and toured the

Canadian coffeehouse circuit before loading up his 1953 Pontiac hearse and heading for Los Angeles. He founded Buffalo Springfield with Stephen Stills and Richie Furay. The band lasted for only two years, but left an indelible imprint on the rock scene.

Following the split, Young embarked on a solo career with *Neil Young* (1969), then teamed with the loud and powerful Crazy Horse for *Everybody Knows This Is Nowhere*. Next came two records with CS&N, interrupted by *After the Goldrush*. In 1972, he landed his first and sole number one single, "Heart of Gold." Many fans consider the album it came from, *Harvest*, to be Young's best.

His most notable albums of the seventies also include *Tonight's the Night* (1975) and *Rust Never Sleeps* (1979). *Decade* (1977) chronicled his best work, both on his own and with his various groups, and still serves as the perfect primer for fans searching for a salad-days sampler.

Young's records for the Geffen label were odd lots indeed. He went computer cyberpunk on *Trans* (1983), slipped on blue suede shoes for the rockabilly-flavored *Everybody's Rockin'* that same year, went country bumpkin on *Old Ways* (1985), reteamed with Crazy Horse for the poorly received *Landing on Water* (1986), released the equally bland *Life* (1987), then formed a rhythm and blues ensemble, the Blue Notes, for *This Note's for You* (1988). In December 1983, Geffen Records accused him of turning in work that "was not commercial in nature and was musically uncharacteristic of Young's previous records."

But in 1989, Young rebounded with *Freedom*, which included what has become something of a signature song, "Rockin' in the Free World." Fans rejoiced at this return to form, which continued into the nineties with *Ragged Glory*, *Harvest Moon*, and the live collection *Weld*. Touring with Young disciples Sonic Youth and Pearl Jam has kept him in the highest regard with the next generation of rock fans. Damned how he does it, but Neil stays Young.

> **Few rockers command as much respect as Canadian Neil Young. His performances in the nineties were as vital as his early days with Buffalo Springfield and his records and tours with Crazy Horse in the seventies.**

EPILOGUE

By the end of the seventies, rock and roll had become a huge industry, concerned mainly with the bottom line. Progressive, free-form radio was a thing of the past. Nearly every station had a regimented playlist. Concerts were arena-size extravaganzas. A souvenir T-shirt cost as much as the ticket. Major record labels ruled the day. Rock stars lived opulently. To many ears, the music wore thin.

A new generation of rock fans had no use for the corporate, comfortable convention that rock had slipped into. After all, rock and roll was originally music to rebel by. Now it was something to rebel against. In came the punk movement. Led by the Ramones in America and the Sex Pistols in England (with a nod to early adventurers Iggy [Pop] and the Stooges, the New York Dolls, and the Velvet Underground), punk returned rock to its roots: short songs played at a frantic pace with no frills and a heavy dose of post-teenage angst. You didn't need money or music lessons to be a punk. Virtuosity took a backseat. This was do-it-yourself music direct from garageland. Enough kids on both sides of the Atlantic took to the underground nature of the new brigade—enough for the mainstream to take notice, but not enough to reach the top of the charts.

The New Wave rockers of the late seventies/early eighties, although born in the punk movement, didn't seem as dangerous or threatening. So new bands like America's Blondie and Talking Heads, England's Police, and Ireland's U2 started to sell a significant number of records. Some held their ground through the eighties and built a huge fan base—groups like U2, REM, and the Cure. But a heavy metal renaissance in the eighties led by outfits like Quiet Riot, Def Leppard, and, later on, Guns N' Roses and Metallica, kept the noisier punks at bay—at least until the early nineties, when a Seattle grunge movement blew sky-high on the strength of two bands: Nirvana and Pearl Jam. To boot, a lot of restless kids turned to rap.

As for the classic rockers, the strong remained vital—Neil Young, for instance—as others either adjusted to VH-1 status, became band managers or record company executives, or fell by the wayside altogether. Many just sat on their assets until the obligatory reunion album or tour beckoned. For most, that last gasp was an embarrassing moment.

After the seventies, the rules changed. The arrival of MTV—Music Television—in 1981 and its immediate success meant that a music video was now as important as the record. In some cases, it was more so. Rock stars became television stars. In the process, rock lost a lot of its mystique and charm. There it is, on your television, twenty-four hours a day. It's as American as baseball and apple pie.

But as long as there are kids, there will be a segment of the music-buying public whose hormones rage a bit faster, whose appetite for entertainment continues to push the limits of popular music a bit further. As time advances, they'll have little use for classic rock, but they'll be after the same kicks that the kids who got caught up in Beatlemania were after, all those years ago.

ROCK AND ROLL HALL OF FAMERS

The Rock and Roll Hall of Fame and Museum in Cleveland, Ohio, honors rock's finest artists, many of them from the classic rock period.

1986 ARTIST INDUCTEES

Chuck Berry, James Brown, Ray Charles, Sam Cooke, Fats Domino, the Everly Brothers, Buddy Holly, Jerry Lee Lewis, Little Richard, Elvis Presley

1987 ARTIST INDUCTEES

The Coasters, Eddie Cochran, Bo Diddley, Aretha Franklin, Marvin Gaye, Bill Haley, B.B. King, Clyde McPhatter, Ricky Nelson, Roy Orbison, Carl Perkins, Smokey Robinson, Big Joe Turner, Muddy Waters, Jackie Wilson

1988 ARTIST INDUCTEES

The Beach Boys, the Beatles, the Drifters, Bob Dylan, the Supremes

1989 ARTIST INDUCTEES

Dion, Otis Redding, the Rolling Stones, the Temptations, Stevie Wonder

ONE-HIT HARRYS

Source: Rock and Roll
Hall of Fame and
Museum, Inc.

1990 ARTIST INDUCTEES

Hank Ballard, Bobby Darin, the Four Seasons, the Four Tops, the Kinks, the Platters, Simon and Garfunkel, the Who

1991 ARTIST INDUCTEES

Lavern Baker, the Byrds, John Lee Hooker, the Impressions, Wilson Pickett, Jimmy Reed, Ike and Tina Turner

1992 ARTIST INDUCTEES

Bobby "Blue" Bland, Booker T. and the MG's, Johnny Cash, the Isley Brothers, the Jimi Hendrix Experience, Sam and Dave, the Yardbirds

1993 ARTIST INDUCTEES

Ruth Brown, Cream, Creedence Clearwater Revival, the Doors, Etta James, Frankie Lymon and the Teenagers, Van Morrison, Sly and the Family Stone

1994 ARTIST INDUCTEES

The Animals, the Band, Duane Eddy, The Grateful Dead, Elton John, John Lennon, Bob Marley, Rod Stewart

The classic rock period is stacked with artists who struck gold with one great song but, for one reason or another, could never repeat their success. Some of these rockers had follow-up hits, but nowhere near as memorable as that great tune. These songs are among the best-loved in classic rock. Long may they be heard and remembered.

"96 Tears," ? and the Mysterians, 1966

"98.6," Keith, 1967

"Baby It's You," Smith, 1969

"Beautiful Sunday," Daniel Boone, 1972

"Chick-A-Boom," Daddy Dewdrop, 1971

"Classical Gas," Mason Williams, 1968

"Dirty Water," Standells, 1966

"Double Shot (of My Baby's Love)," Swingin' Medallions, 1966

"Do You Know What I Mean," Lee Michaels, 1971

"Elusive Butterfly," Bob Lind, 1966

"Everlasting Love," Carl Carlton, 1974

"Expressway to Your Heart," Soul Survivors, 1967

"A Fifth of Beethoven," Walter Murphy, 1976

"Fire," The Crazy World of Arthur Brown, 1968

"Fooled Around and Fell in Love," Elvin Bishop, 1976

"Get It On," Chase, 1971

"Gimme Dat Ding," The Pipkins, 1970

"Green-Eyed Lady," Sugarloaf, 1970

"Hey Joe," Leaves, 1966

"Hooked on a Feeling," Blue Swede, 1974

"How Do You Do?" Mouth & MacNeal, 1972

"I Got a Line on You," Spirit, 1969

"I Had Too Much to Dream (Last Night)," Electric Prunes, 1967

"Indiana Wants Me," R. Dean Taylor, 1970

"In the Summertime," Mungo Jerry, 1970

"Liar, Liar," Castaways, 1965

"Little Bit o' Soul," Music Explosion, 1967

"Love Grows (Where My Rosemary Goes)," Edison Lighthouse, 1970

"Ma Belle Amie," Tee Set, 1970

"Me and You and a Dog Named Boo," Lobo, 1971

"More Today Than Yesterday," Spiral Starecase, 1969

"My Baby Loves Lovin'," White Plains, 1970

"Na Na Hey Hey Kiss Him Goodbye," Steam, 1969

"Nobody but Me," Human Beinz, 1968

"One Fine Morning," Lighthouse, 1971

"One Toke Over the Line," Brewer & Shipley, 1971

"Pictures of Matchstick Men," Status Quo, 1968

"Please Come to Boston," Dave Loggins, 1974

"Psychotic Reaction," Count Five, 1966

"The Rapper," Jaggerz, 1970

"Rock and Roll Part 2," Gary Glitter, 1972

"Rock On," David Essex, 1974

"San Francisco (Be Sure to Wear Flowers in Your Hair)," Scott McKenzie, 1967

"Seasons in the Sun," Terry Jacks, 1974

"Signs," Five Man Electrical Band, 1971

"Smile a Little Smile for Me," Flying Machine, 1969

"Something in the Air," Thunderclap Newman, 1969

"Spirit in the Sky," Norman Greenbaum, 1970

"Sunshine," Jonathan Edwards, 1972

"Surfin' Bird," Trashmen, 1964

"Sweet Soul Music," Arthur Conley, 1967

"Talk Talk," Music Machine, 1966

"Tighter, Tighter," Alive and Kicking, 1970

"Time Won't Let Me," Outsiders, 1966

"United We Stand," Brotherhood of Man, 1970

"Venus," Shocking Blue, 1970

"Western Union," Five Americans, 1967

"Winchester Cathedral," New Vaudeville Band, 1966

"You Were on My Mind," We Five, 1965

THE TOP FIFTY CLASSIC ROCK SONGS OF ALL TIME

Here are the fifty most-played songs on classic rock radio, according to Jacobs Media, a radio industry consultant and research firm.

1. "Stairway to Heaven," Led Zeppelin
2. "Dream On," Aerosmith
3. "In the Air Tonight," Phil Collins
4. "Turn the Page," Bob Seger
5. "You Can't Always Get What You Want," Rolling Stones
6. "Hotel California," Eagles
7. "Time," Pink Floyd
8. "Sweet Emotion," Aerosmith
9. "Wonderful Tonight," Eric Clapton
10. "Free Bird," Lynyrd Skynyrd
11. "Carry On Wayward Son," Kansas
12. "Over the Hills and Far Away," Led Zeppelin
13. "Your Song," Elton John
14. "Brain Damage/Eclipse," Pink Floyd
15. "Magic Carpet Ride," Steppenwolf
16. "Imagine," John Lennon
17. "Foreplay/Long Time," Boston
18. "Black Dog," Led Zeppelin
19. "Bad Company," Bad Company
20. "Kashmir," Led Zeppelin
21. "Candle in the Wind," Elton John
22. "Another Brick in the Wall (Part II)," Pink Floyd
23. "Brown Eyed Girl," Van Morrison
24. "Sweet Home Alabama," Lynyrd Skynyrd
25. "Maybe I'm Amazed," Paul McCartney
26. "I Still Haven't Found What I'm Looking For," U2
27. "Maggie May," Rod Stewart
28. "Bad to the Bone," George Thorogood
29. "Beast of Burden," Rolling Stones
30. "Behind Blue Eyes," Who
31. "Tiny Dancer," Elton John
32. "Money," Pink Floyd
33. "For What It's Worth," Buffalo Springfield
34. "Hey You," Pink Floyd
35. "White Room," Cream
36. "Cocaine," Eric Clapton
37. "Rocket Man," Elton John
38. "More Than a Feeling," Boston
39. "Satisfaction," Rolling Stones
40. "Ramble On," Led Zeppelin
41. "(Sittin' on) The Dock of the Bay," Otis Redding
42. "Faithfully," Journey
43. "Comfortably Numb," Pink Floyd
44. "Have You Ever Seen the Rain," Creedence Clearwater Revival
45. "Born to Be Wild," Steppenwolf
46. "Wish You Were Here," Pink Floyd
47. "You Shook Me All Night Long," AC/DC
48. "Already Gone," Eagles
49. "Blinded by the Light," Manfred Mann
50. "Layla," Derek and the Dominoes

Reprinted by permission of Jacobs Media Research, Inc.

Further Reading

Bane, Michael. *Who's Who in Rock*. New York: Facts on File, Inc., 1981.

Charlesworth, Chris. *A-Z of Rock Guitarists*. London: Proteus Books, 1982.

———. *The Who: The Illustrated Biography*. London: Omnibus Press, 1982.

Christgau, Robert. *Christgau's Record Guide: Rock Albums of the Seventies*. New Haven, Conn.: Ticknor & Fields, 1981.

Clifford, Mike. *The Harmony Illustrated Encyclopedia of Rock*. New York: Harmony Books, 1983.

Coleman, Ray. *Lennon: The Definitive Biography*. New York: Harper Perennial, 1992.

Cooper, Michael, and Terry Southern. *The Early Stones: Legendary Photographs of a Band in the Making, 1963–1973*. New York: Hyperion, 1992.

Dalton, David, and Lenny Kaye. *Rock 100*. New York: Grosset & Dunlap, 1977.

Dawson, Jim, and Steve Propes. *What Was the First Rock 'n' Roll Record?* Winchester, Mass.: Faber and Faber, 1992.

DeCurtis, Anthony, and James Henke with Holly George-Warren. *Rolling Stone Album Guide*. New York: Random House, 1992.

Densmore, John. *Riders on the Storm*. New York: Delacorte Press, 1990.

Des Barres, Pamela. *I'm With the Band: Confessions of a Groupie*. New York: Jove Books, 1988.

Dolgins, Adam. *Rock Names*. New York: Citadel Press, 1993.

Draper, Robert. *Rolling Stone Magazine: The Uncensored History*. New York: Doubleday, 1990.

Eisen, Jonathan. *The Age of Rock*. New York: Vintage Books, 1969.

Flanagan, Bill. *Written in My Soul*. Chicago: Contemporary Books, 1986.

Flaum, Eric. *The Encyclopedia of Mythology*. Philadelphia: Courage Books, 1993.

Gaines, Steven. *Heroes and Villains: The True Story of the Beach Boys*. New York: Signet, 1986.

Gambaccini, Paul. *Masters of Rock*. London: BBC-Omnibus Press, 1982.

Garr, Gillian. *She's a Rebel: The History of Women in Rock and Roll*. Seattle: Seal Press, 1992.

Giuliano, Geoffrey. *Blackbird: The Life and Times of Paul McCartney*. New York: Dutton, 1991.

———. *Dark Horse: The Private Life of George Harrison*. New York: Plume/Penguin, 1991.

Graham, Bill, and Robert Greenfield. *Bill Graham Presents: My Life Inside Rock and Out*. New York: Delta, 1992.

Heylin, Clinton. *Bob Dylan: Behind the Shades*. New York: Summit Books, 1991.

Holland, Ted. *This Day in African-American Music*. San Francisco: Pomegranate Artbooks, 1993.

Lewisohn, Mark. *The Complete Beatles Chronicle*. New York: Harmony Books, 1992.

Lisciandro, Frank. *Morrison: A Feast of Friends*. New York: Warner Books, 1991.

Maltin, Leonard. *Leonard Maltin's TV Movies and Video Guide, 1988 Edition*. New York: Signet, 1987.

Marks, Peter. "Recalling the Screams Heard Round the World," *New York Times*, February 6, 1994.

Marsh, Dave. *Born to Run: The Bruce Springsteen Story*. Garden City, N.Y.: Doubleday/Dolphin, 1979.

Miller, Jim. *The Rolling Stone Illustrated History of Rock & Roll*. New York: Random House/Rolling Stone Press, 1980.

Murray, Charles Shaar. *Crosstown Traffic: Jimi Hendrix and the Post-War Rock 'n' Roll Revolution*. New York: St. Martin's Press, 1989.

Norman, Philip. *Shout! The Beatles in Their Generation*. New York: Fireside, 1981.

Pareles, Jon, and Patricia Romanowski. *The Rolling Stone Encyclopedia of Rock & Roll*. New York: Rolling Stone Press/Summit Books, 1983.

Pawlowski, Gareth L. *How They Became the Beatles*. New York: E.P. Dutton, 1989.

Robbins, Ira A. *The New Trouser Press Record Guide*. New York: Collier Books, 1989.

Roberty, Marc. *Eric Clapton: The Complete Recording Sessions, 1963–1992*. New York: St. Martin's Press, 1993.

———. *Slowhand: The Life and Music of Eric Clapton*. New York: Crown Trade Paperbacks, 1993.

Rolling Stone, Editors. *Rock Almanac: The Chronicles of Rock & Roll*. New York: Rolling Stone Press/Collier Books, 1983.

———. *The Rolling Stone Interviews: The 1980s*. Rolling Stone Press/St. Martin's Press, 1989.

Schaffner, Nicholas. *The British Invasion*. New York: McGraw-Hill, 1983.

Wade, Dorothy, and Justine Picardie. *Music Man: Ahmet Ertegun, Atlantic Records and the Triumph of Rock 'n' Roll*. New York: W.W. Norton & Company, 1990.

Ward, Ed, Geoffrey Stokes, and Ken Tucker. *Rock of Ages: The Rolling Stone History of Rock & Roll*. New York: Rolling Stone Press/Summit Press, 1986.

Whitburn, Joel. *The Billboard Book of Top 40 Hits*. New York: Billboard Books/Wastson-Guptill Publications, 1989.

White, Timothy. *Rock Lives: Profiles and Interviews*. New York: Henry Holt and Company, 1990.

Photography Credits

© **FPG International**: p. 12 both, 14; © **Bob Peterson**: p. 59, 66 both, 67; © **Terry Strom**: p. 29 r

© **Globe Photos**: p. 15, 31, 32, 39, 52, 55, 72, 78, 107, 133; © **Mark Allan/Alpha**: p. 76, 127; © **Heilemann/Camera Press**: p. 29 l; © **Chris Harris**: p. 142; © **Richard Imrie**: p. 84 r; © **Walter Iooss**: p. 48 l; © **Bruce McBroom**: p. 57; © **Richard Polak**: p. 138 l; © **George Rodriquez**: p . 83; © **J. Stevens/Photo Trends**: p. 75 m

© **Gray-Zlozower**: p. 77 both, 89, 91

© **Jason Laure**: p. 10 l, 22 l

© **London Features**: p. 30 l, 96

© **Michael Ochs Archive**: p.37

© **Photofeatures International**: © **Andre Csillag**: p. 147 l; © **Chris Walter**: p. 7, 53, 97, 150

Photofest: p. 49, 64 l

© **Retna Ltd.**: p. 35, 82; © **John Atashian**: p. 106; © **Joel Axelrad**: p. 101; © **Ken Berard**: p. 58 l; © **George Bodnar**: p. 128, 129; ©**Adrian Boot**: p. 26 l, 27; © **David Corio**: p. 123; © **Fin Costello**: p. 74 r, 81, 132; © **Arthur D'Amario**: p. 75 l; © **Bob Freeman**: p. 13; © **Gary Gershoff**: p. 117, 145 r; © **Andrew Kent**: p. 22 r, 84 l, 87, 103, 105, 130; © **Janet Macoskor**: p. 114 l; © **Michael Putland**: p. 17, 18, 21 r, 33, 38, 40 all, 44 l, 48 r, 54, 56, 69, 85, 90, 93, 95, 110, 111, 125 m,

146; © **David Redfern**: p. 24, 34, 41, 71, 100, 116, 152 l; © **Tom Reusche**: p. 126 l; © **Chieko Sano**: p. 114 r; ©**Barry Schultz**: p. 6, 86; © **Peter Smith**: p. 143; © **Anthony Stern**: p. 23; © **Ray Stevenson**: p. 11; © **Chris Walter**: p. 73; © **Scott Weiner**: p. 148 l; © **Gary Weston**: p. 104 l; © **Rocky Widner**: p. 10 r, 19 r, 104 r, 112

© **Joe Sia**: p. 43

Star File: p. 92 r, 144; © **Richard E. Aaron/Thunder Thumbs**: p. 74 l, 102, 147 r; © **Bob Alford**: p. 113; © **Lydia Criss**: p. 151; © **Ron Delany**: p. 61, 62; © **Bob Gruen**: p. 28 l, 30 r, 75 r, 131; © **Mark Harlan**: p. 68; © **Steve Joester**: p. 80, 125 l, 135, 141; © **Ken**

Kaminsky: p. 145 l; © **Larry Kaplan**: p. 136, 152 r; © **Elliott Landy**: p. 9, 46, 60, 64 r, 92 l, 94, 98; © **Bob Leafe**: p. 70 r; © **John Lee**: p. 63, 108; © **Charles Martin**: p. 148 r; © **Jeff Mayer**: p. 134; © **Pictorial Press Limited**: p. 21 l, 42, 50, 58 r, 70 l; © **Chuck Pulin**: p. 2 r, 125 r; © **Mick Rock**: p. 26 r, 115, 122; © **David Seelig**: p. 138 r, 139; © **Gene Shaw**: p. 126 r; © **Geoffrey Thomas**: p. 119

© **Neil Zlozower**: p. 2 l, 19 l, 44 r, 45 both, 79, 109, 118, 120, 121, 124, 137, 140

Directional key: l—left, r—right, b—bottom, t—top, m—middle

Index